The Salon & the 'S' Word

Success

Mike Vallance

SalonStudies

The Salon & the 'S' Word – Success

The SalonStudies logo is a registered trademark used herein under license.

For more information, contact SalonStudies Ltd. 145-157, St John Street. London ECIV 4PW or visit us at http://www.salonstudies.com

British Library Cataloguing-in-Publication Data
A catalogue record for this book is available from the British Library

ISBN: 978-0-9929695-2-3

First edition published 2015 by SalonStudies Ltd.

Printed by CreateSpace, An Amazon.com Company

Other titles by the editor

Mirrored Vision - Finding Customers Keeping Clients - Martin Green
ISBN 978-0-9929695-0-9
Published by SalonStudies - 2014

Ready for Hairdressing Workbook - Martin Green
ISBN 978-0-9929695-1-6
Published by SalonStudies - 2015

Salon Management: - Martin Green
ISBN 978-1-86152-660-1
Published by Thomson - First printed - 2001
reprinted 2005 & 2007 by Thomson learning

Hairdressing & Barbering - The Foundations: The Official Guide to
Hairdressing & Barbering NVQ at Level 2 7e - Martin Green
ISBN 978-1-4080-7110-6
Published by Cengage Learning - 2013

Hairdressing & Barbering - The Foundations: The Official Guide to
Hairdressing & Barbering VRQ at Level 2 1e - Martin Green
ISBN 978-1-4080-7111-3
Published by Cengage Learning - 2013

Professional Hairdressing: - The Official Guide to Hairdressing S/NVQ at
Level 3 Revised 6e - Martin Green & Leo Palladino
ISBN 978-1-4080-3981-6
Published by Cengage Learning - 2011

Begin Hairdressing & Barbering: The Official Guide to Hairdressing &
Barbering NVQ at Level 1 3e - Martin Green
ISBN 978-1-4080-3979-3
Published by Cengage Learning - 2011

The Pocket Guide to Key Terms for Hairdressing: Levels 1,2&3 Martin Green
ISBN 978-1-4080-6041-4
Published by Cengage Learning EMEA - 2012

Acknowledgements

The author and publisher would like to thank the following people and organizations for their assistance in the production of this book.

- Carol Alsop
- Paul Cooper
- Cat Holbrook
- Chester Graham
- TypeCraft Ltd
- Freestyle Design Ltd
- CreateSpace

....

First and foremost, I would like to thank my wife Cindy, 'Cinders,' for her unfailing support, and encouragement while working on this project. I would also like to thank Martin for his guidance in making this publication a reality. Finally, a thanks to all the others that I had the good fortune to work with; whom without, I would not have had the experience to draw upon.
- Mike Vallance -

Editor's foreword

Finding passion in this industry is easy, everyone whoever made that transition from stylist to a salon owner has it. We all started out with similar intentions and in order to be the best we felt that we needed to beat the rest. Well, that is true in some respects, but in an industry that relies on respect; along with consistent good service, you need to find something else. Something that gives you the edge without removing the personality that everyone admires and wants to be with, yes, we all want to be liked, but management is a lonely and isolated position.

So, in taking that step, passion takes on a new meaning. It's not just your enthusiasm, self-motivation and continuing good service that is in question, it's taking up the challenge of managing that passion within others.

I have admired the passion that Mike Vallance demonstrates in all his communications with his professional contacts across the globe. Sometimes contributing his knowledge and experience through advice, other times acting as arbitrator between groups and entities who feel polarized in their beliefs, values and opinions.

Regardless of their standpoints, they all rely on his judgment, and you will find that his passion still *burns through* and will reach out and touch you in this book.

Martin Green

Contents

Contents *cont.*

1

INTRODUCTION

Introduction, where do I start? It is one thing to set out with a clear idea of what you want to achieve in life, but for us in the hair business, it does not seem to work out like that. In my experience, the people that work in our industry have had a fairly checkered background and have trodden through all sorts of terrain to get where they are. They say that you learn by experience, well if that is true, how many mistakes do you need to make before you get it all, right, a lifetime's worth?

What if you could get an insight into what to expect and without having to experience all the challenges personally? Well, perhaps by doing what you do best, you can use your powers of observation and learn from the experiences of another.

We can all turn our hands to most things, but being able to excel at something with passion and deep interest; as a career choice, must be very special. If you think back to when you set out, did you have any idea of how hard it was going to be, or what to expect?

Opportunities will always present them self and when they do we have a choice take up the challenge or just play safe.

I also believe that as we develop skills and gain knowledge that we are duty bound to share and pass it on. If we do not, then everything we have learned is wasted.

A career in hairdressing can offer so much more than a routine nine to five job. It can be diverse and challenging; however, the rewards and potential for success are boundless. If you are conscientious and

hard working then you are equipped to explore the many opportunities that this industry can offer.

This book is my opportunity to pass on and share with you some of my knowledge and experience in the hope of inspiring you to put a little time aside for your personal quest.

"It will be a journey that will raise questions, encourage new thinking and open a debate on some key issues relating to your salon and our industry. There are so many topics that remain overlooked and yet the fundamental aspects of salon and business success, such as stability; security, growth and profitability all depend upon them."

....

"At this point, I would like to thank Martin Green for this amazing opportunity.".

....

How did I get into hairdressing?

"In writing this book, it is my hope that I can share my experiences, my journey in this amazing industry, but also to inspire all those who struggle with learning or retaining information."

How can a school leaver at the seasoned age of 15, possibly know what they want to do with, and in their working life? Well, that was the thoughts that challenged me when I started my career back in 1973. At that time, there were only two possible routes to take. The first if you passed your GCSEs would lead on to further or higher education, or the second that leads the (supposedly) underachievers into routine jobs or technical apprenticeships.

Did I know what I wanted to do? No! The only thing I knew was that I hated school; the exams had always been a struggle for me, so I wanted out, I wanted to start work and learn a trade.

Taking up hairdressing and being a hairstylist has always been a career option for those considered as 'academically challenged'. Well, that was how I thought of myself; my sisters' got all the brains. (I have to include this, as I write this introduction to inspire all those who struggle with learning and retaining information.) I learned much later in life that I was dyslexic, and although not considered a barrier to learning now; it was not recognized or supported then.

We can all learn and retain information providing that the way in which we learn, suits our needs. I didn't start out with the intention of being an educator; that came much later, but my learning experiences made me adaptable to other peoples' needs. As each generation moves on and through our industry, the environment changes and necessitates the person to change as well.

The hair stylist of today is a creative professional with excellent communication skills. They need to be IT 'savvy,' understand the positive and negative aspects of social media and above all, be able to understand what working in a personal service industry means.

I started a hairdressing apprenticeship in June 1973 in a *Knightsbridge* salon in London. It was an exciting time in the business when everything was changing. *Vidal Sassoon* had recently become a 'household' name by moving the shampoo and set into the precision cut and blow-dry.

Fashions will always come and go, but fundamental changes to the way in which people style their hair may only happen once in a lifetime. It was a time packed with energy and enthusiasm where stylists competed to have their work published in Vogue, and the standards in training were stringent but pivotal in aspiring those professionals.

Just starting....

My first job was a real 'eye-opener;' the first six months were hard, not knowing what I should be doing, what I should be saying or how I should be saying it. My school memories were a world apart from all that shampooing, sweeping up, cleaning and assisting stylists. Working through from Monday to Saturday and finishing around two o'clock, to then get paid and have nothing to show for it. I survived on the tips; that was one of the benefits of working in a 'smarter' part of the city; all those wealthy women!

Even then, I could see the potential; if I could master the techniques, the possibilities were there. I realized pretty quickly that in order to be successful in our industry, you have to be liked and like other people.

The early days (1973 – 1974)

From the outset, I was told that cutting is everything and learning to cut would come in the latter part of my training. So get over it and on with it! Those top salon stylists worked so quickly; it made everything look easy.

"The quickness of the hand deceives the eye." I don't know where that quote came from, but oh so true. I soon learned that everything looks simple – yes, when you know how! Holding, folding, sectioning and fastening, gripping and smoothing, but above all, neatness and speed.

The first real ordeal for a trainee: **perm winds and brush control!**

Dexterity is something that you have; it cannot be learned and without it hairdressing is an uphill challenge. I remember that first perm wind, trying to get the sectioning right with the correct mesh width, thickness, tension, and then add an end paper! Then after all that and eventually getting the first one right, you have to repeat the process another sixty times! I thought that I was training for the circus, all that juggling with end papers, perming rods, pin-tail combs and fastening rubbers, and after picking one up you can't put it back down. Trying to wind with an even tension, placing the end paper correctly, so that the free edges extend just enough to help wind in the rod, but without buckling the hair. It took hours. Eventually, after lots of practice it got easier, I got quicker, I was even allowed to use perm lotion instead of water!

Blow-drying was a similar ordeal; it looked easy but once again when an item is picked up; it was never put down. How many hands do you need? I remember having to hold the hair dryer in one hand and a radial brush in the other, then take new sections whilst keeping the worked hair smooth. Now place the damp hair evenly across the surface of the brush, and then dry it with an even tension whilst not burning the hair or the client!

"I am not going to go on about my training, but in reflection, however tough it seemed it was worth it. "

The consummate trainee

Towards the end of my training I was offered a great opportunity, it meant leaving the one place that felt safe, but I wanted more. I had a chance to finish my training in a top West End salon with some of the most passionate creatives that the industry had to offer. It was the chance of a lifetime; it would be hard, and it meant lower pay and back to 'boot camp.' And with their very high expectations only a few ever survive, but I had to take it and never looked back.

Where was it? **Leonard of Mayfair**

It got me into new circles, top stylists, celebrities, and the glitterati. I have arrived!

Twiggy walking in on the arm of **Justin de Villeneuve** and **Lulu** checking out the music press whilst having her hair done, I was star-struck! **Daniel Galvin, John Frieda, Clifford Stafford, Nicky Clark, Barry Wilde**. It was surreal; this is my induction into hedonistic hairdressing back in that primordial time when '*champers*' or rather shampoo, meant something else.

Following on from the revolution and revelations that changed everything in the 60s, it created a new creative landscape for the 70's. It was a great time to be hairdressing, and that was because all of those big names had created a new benchmark and set a new foundation for an industry that has never looked back.

Smith & Gardner, *London, 1974-1986*

Junior stylist/Manager /Director
....

I progressed from a junior stylist to a manager and then on to company director. S&G was where I really got to learn about developing a clientele, about building relationships, creating customer loyalty and regular, repeat business.

South of the River, *London, 1986-1989*

Proprietor
....

My first salon, my venture, it was a time of *big shoulder pads* and *big ideas*, time to take risks. I took a risk in opening in an 'up-and-coming' area; it was on the brink of taking off. The hard work and challenges were nothing compared to the rewards for creating a unique environment and with a team of true international talent.

The salon was fully booked from day one, my truly amazing and supportive clients followed me to a new location, yet without them, this could so easily have gone wrong. As the business grew, we added a beauty room, a barbering section; it was one of the first real salon spas. The business developed with the support of a team of talented, international stylists.

Then to Canada...

Renaldo's, *Ottawa/Canada, 1989–1993* Stylist

Avant Garde, *Vancouver/ Canada 1997-2000*

Artistic team member / Platform & stage artist

The Gallery Salon, *Victoria, 2000*

Stylist/ Educator/ Platform artist,

L'anza *Professional Hair Products/ Canada 2000-2005*

West Coast Senior Educator & Platform Artist

John Paul Salon, *Victoria, 2001-2002*

Stylist/Artistic Team, Platform Artist

M.V. Hair Design, *Victoria, 2003-2008* Proprietor

My move to Canada was a roller coaster, I had gone from owning a salon, back to working for some else. A huge readjustment, but the team in Ottawa was very accommodating, they liked me, my skills, and my approach to working with clients. We learned lessons from one another, a truly international collaboration. Ottawa proved to be the perfect introduction to the Canadian hairdressing scene.

Vancouver was probably my biggest challenge yet, and working for an internationally acclaimed stylist; *John Paul Holt*, I was now part of the creative team that wanted to be the best and 'push the envelope' on hair design. *Deja-vu*, this was reminiscent of my early beginnings; it was a salon with true passion and driven by someone with vision and focus. It was a very competitive environment, and I found this hard to start with, but learned to embrace the concept of being involved in shows, stage work and sometimes even winning!

My personal highlights during this time were

▶ Runner up in L'Oreal Color trophy, Silver Medal winner, 1999

▶ Allied Beauty Association (ABA) center stage show, Vancouver 1998

▶ Alternative hair show, Chicago, 1998

▶ Alternative hair show, Royal Albert Hall, London, 1997

▶ Full work history and bio - https://www.linkedin.com/in/mikevallanceb2mr

And now...

Consultant: *B2MR salon consultancy /online support*

"Coming back to England in 2008 was a big decision and having been away for around 20 years, it was starting over making your contacts and connection. It was creating an online presence, this involved learning about social media and the power of networking. I had to start again."

A thought to share

My career has taken many twists and turns, and this has enabled me to achieve things that would be impossible had I stayed in one place. It has allowed me to be objective about an industry that spends more time looking outwards rather than inwards, and that is the starting point of this book.

Remember, before we can go forwards we sometimes have to go backwards, and that is a tough decision for anyone to take. As hairdressers, we often spend our time worrying about the things beyond the horizon, the things that we cannot see or have not yet happened. Focus upon the things that you can change or do now, and leave all the worrying about things like; the client with one-length hair down her back who is having highlights, - until she arrives.

"Oh, answer that call, I think she's about to cancel."

"I strongly urge you to take up the opportunity to connect with the luminaries within our industry. You will find them to be like-minded professionals who have a thirst for knowledge and passion for excellence. They are hairdressers who want to make a difference, raise standards and tackle the issues facing our industry today. Underlying all this is a common energy that strives to deliver the best service, offers the most creative solutions and helps us prevent those clients from cancelling!"

SalonStudies
Hair Stylist's Guides

2

HOW WELL DO YOU KNOW YOUR CLIENTS?

How well do you know your customers?

We know that if customers are dissatisfied with the service they receive, or the products that they buy, they will switch to another provider or source. We also know that without customers, a business will cease trading. Yes, it is simple to understand, and it does have a critical outcome.

How do we recognize a potential customer?

A quick, rash response would be;

"We don't need to because they are all potential customers."

In some respects, that comment is true, and we all have to speculate in order to accumulate. However, it can be an expensive way of building a clientèle as it costs twenty times more to find a new customer than it does to keep an existing one.

It is a shocking fact that so much money can be wasted in trying to find new customers and in an industry made up of small businesses; not many have any to throw away.

Good business managers do not take unnecessary risks; they evaluate their services, staffing and products so that they can tailor their business offering to a specific customer profile. That profile or

market is a true representation of the type of customer that generates their income. Therefore, without wasting resources in trying to be all things to all people, they have a smaller scope and a clearer view of what matters.

You need to define your target market so that you do not waste your time and money looking for people who are looking elsewhere. Even with the best intentions, you will not be able to keep a client who is constantly looking out the window. There is a simple analogy for this common misconception:

"It is pointless making a Roll-Royce for people with a 'push-bike' income."

In other words, it is pointless creating a salon with lavish fittings and décor and providing a first-class service if your main target market cannot afford your services. They may find the ambience and experience wonderful, but if they are stretching themselves to afford your tariffs, then you will lose them in the end!

The secret for developing a successful business is knowing the profile of the customer that you are aiming at and then finding the correct communications channels/methods for reaching them.

Does 'class' matter?

In many spheres, class does matter. A person's background and upbringing have a lot to do with their associations and people with whom they have an affinity. The 'old boys' network was the only way in which people from certain private schools and colleges would find others who could act or work for them in a professional capacity. For example, Accountants, Lawyers, Financial Services, Investments etc..

Similarly, a closed group like *The Masons* would identify people that they wanted to be involved in their membership and approach them directly by personal invite. This exclusivity was not just a thing of the *Western World* either; many countries try to define and distinguish between people at different levels on the social scale, and this has been happening for thousands of years.

Latterly, class distinctions are not linked to birthrights, audible accents, or geography, they are defined by money. That does not necessarily mean disposable income either; it is one thing having a lot of money and quite another having access to lots of money.

We now live in a time-frame where no one has a private life, everyone is using social media and believing what they read and hear. Some people use social media as a way of marketing themselves the majority use it to tell everyone else what they are doing and the two practices are very different.

So, if social classes are defined by amounts of money, does that matter to you and your clients? **Fortunately not.**

Hairdressing is one of the personal services that is unaffected by the ability to do a good job, for anyone and from any background. It is more to do with the way that communication takes place between different clients that make all the difference.

A successful hairdresser can pitch at any level; they are as comfortable with the Lords and Ladies of the world, as they are with beggars and buskers. At the point where hairdressers try to distinguish between people within their clientèle, things will inevitably go wrong.

Socio-economic categories

The divisions between social classes are blurred, and the differences between lower, middle and upper class are often (wrongly) assumed. However, the mechanisms for measuring differences within people's disposable income are here to stay.

From a marketer's standpoint, this is the way that consumers are grouped, and each country has a system for profiling people into wealth bands or ranges. In the UK, the *ABC1* demographic classifications refer to the social grade definitions, which are used to describe, measure and classify people of different social grades or income and earnings levels.

The table below shows a typical breakdown of socioeconomic categories:

Social Grade	Social Status	Occupation
A	*Upper middle class*	Higher managerial, administrative or professional
B	*Middle class*	Intermediate managerial, administrative or professional
C1	*Lower middle class*	Supervisory or clerical, junior managerial, administrative or professional
C2	*Skilled working class*	Skilled manual workers
D	*Working class*	Semi and unskilled manual workers
E	*Those at lowest level of subsistence*	State pensioners or widows (no other earner), casual or lowest grade workers

Admittedly, the groupings can be broken down further, but as a general guide this provides a starting place for the marketer. The table overleaf provides a synopsis for current demographic trends for all sorts of marketing plans and schemes.

The classifications shown in the first table do not show any figurative data in relation to income, although some adaptations to this basic profiling will give some value ranges. For our purposes, this is not necessary as we are looking at general groupings.

ABC1 demographic trends

Spending patterns:	Food:	Housing:
In the UK statistics reveal that the past few years have seen a steady increase in the number of adults who fall in the A, B and C1 socio-economic group. This can be attributed to various factors such as the changes in the economic conditions, rise in educational opportunities and changing employment patterns across the globe. All these factors have resulted in a shift of focus from the traditional 'blue collar' jobs to those in the 'knowledge professions.' The rise in the ABC1 social grade, and the subsequent increase in spending power, has had a strong impact across industries and markets in the UK.	Historically, the ABC1 consumers have been ready to pay more for their food as compared to the people in the lower social grade. Figures point to the fact that since 1999, ABC1 consumers have strongly been influencing on many of the trends within the food market. This trend is not just based on higher affluence but also on other factors such as a greater awareness of health issues and ethical concerns relating to food. Also online shopping has been a very strong driving force for increased spending on premium food products. But trends now show that during the present economic crisis, manufacturers and retailers would find it harder to charge a premium on top of the already inflated basic food prices as the ABC1 consumers would not really be willing to pay more.	In the times of the housing boom in the UK, it was the ABC1 consumers who drove the buy-to-let market by investing in property as an alternative to pensions or other financial investments. The 'correction in prices' in the housing market in 2008 will have deep repercussions for the home-related products market. Studies reveal that although consumers in the A and B groups are unlikely to change their spending habits in the prevalent uncertainties in the market, those falling in the C1 would definitely change theirs to weather the crisis.

2.02 - Source: abc1demographic

Take a few moments to look at these and think about where your salon finds a realistic fit with its customers. You might find that you and your team have clients that are representative across several groups. That is fine and in many ways expectable.

For example, when you think of the variety of different supermarkets that there are, it is far easier to position their customers into the different economic categories. It does not mean that someone from an 'A' listed demographic should not, or would not buy from a supermarket that is targeting the 'D' list demographic.

On the contrary, the wealthy people did not get rich by throwing their money away; they will make savings wherever they can. When it comes to well-known branded goods, why should they pay more than they have to for things that they wanted and were going to buy?

Hairdressing is similar in many ways but very different in others and to demonstrate this there is one sobering fact about retailing that many hairdressers will find quite challenging.

In order to be successful:

" Businesses should charge their customers as much as they are willing to pay."

What goes through the mind of the client who can obviously afford more than you are charging? - Who is the winner and who is the loser? This type of client is neither a true reflection of your clientèle or your target market.

However, there will be many others that *love* the things that you do for them, even though they can hardly afford your prices or the regular upkeep of their hair at home.

You are aware of this, but what can you do about it?

Nothing, you cannot change the level of quality that you and your team provide. You can only change the way you offer your services by having different staff working together with differing abilities, and when combined, they provide a reasonable quality matching the value for what you are charging.

Many hair stylists fall into the trap of over-delivering, and this is a very gray area that is difficult to quantify or evaluate. Who is the winner and who is the loser? It is so much easier when it comes to selling products as they are a standardized commodity that have set prices, regardless who buys them.

Does my salon's image matter?

Yes, it does, and this has a lot to do with branding or brand image. - The things that people associate with your business, the products that you use and the products that you sell. However, branding is covered comprehensively in Chapter 4 (pgs 71-92) and you can find out more about this topic another time.

"We have to change our customers' habits."

People are naturally creatures of routine; we do things habitually because we find it easier to live that way. We do things in a repeated pattern and organized way because instinctively, we know that it makes our day-to-day lives easier. Whereas living in chaos might be exciting and fun for a short while, it is challenging and uncomfortable in the long-term and drains our energy very quickly.

Does anything else affect customer choice?

The quickest way to get someone to change a habit is by giving them a compelling reason. The action of winning them over is like *waving a magic wand*. For example, if a new client is thrilled with their final effect, you show them something really personal and important to them.

There is one aspect that affects all of your potential customers; in fact, it is one of the main differences between a customer and a client.

The way that you conjure up ideas and deliver the effect before their eyes makes them feel that they could achieve it themselves.

How would you define the difference between a customer and a client? You might be thinking: *"It is something to do with providing a professional service, or providing professional advice."* You could also say *"it is looking after someone's hair on a regular repeated basis."*

The outcome from this leads to you gaining a new client, and they develop a new habit.

Both of these answers are correct, but in order to be able to get to the point where we can do any of these, we have to do something really difficult first:

Not quite, the impact of doing their hair is one thing; it makes them believe that if you do it, so can they. Most people have little, or no understanding of the technical knowledge and expertise that you spent years to learn. You have made it look so simple - therefore it must be easy!

Then you take the time to explain how they can maintain their hair themselves at home and find that on their next visit they say. *"I couldn't get it to look like you did."*

From the work that you did they develop a new habit. You are added to their list of supporting professionals, but they carry on trying to style their hair, in the same way as before. i.e. using the same equipment, the same products and the same procedures.

If you keep doing things in the same ways, you get the same results.
(Good or bad!)

It is relatively easy to make that first initial impact upon someone else, but far harder when trying to sustain it. If you look at the following illustration, you can imagine that in order to keep the momentum in business, you have to **"ride on the crest of the wave"** just to stay on top. Going with the flow is not enough and no-one will be throwing you a lifeline.

2.04

So where do I begin?

If you know your target market, you will understand their needs and the things that will ultimately drive them to your door. For further information. (See "*macro-trends*" pgs. 80-82)

Therefore, you need to use the socioeconomic groupings to establish your market, but do not make the mistake of overrating your salon or your team's capabilities.

You could look at it another way, where are you located – what is the nature of neighboring businesses? You may be aiming at the higher end of the demographics and the charity shop next door seems to be attracting some well-heeled customers too. But they may be people who are just charitable by nature, or are they just looking for bargains?

Your geographical location means a lot, and although it may be your first salon, your clients will want to follow you wherever you go. (Even if that means dragging them down to the lower end of the High Street.) You may get away with it for a couple of years, but unless you see it as a stepping-stone to where you really want to be, many will drift away over time.

Think about your clients and the discussions that you have had. What sorts of things do they like to buy, where do they go, what do they like doing? Do not just think about your favorites either you need a cross-section that is representative of the total clientèle.

Then get a sheet of paper and complete the information in the table below.

Remember - you are looking for patterns that will inevitably reveal how others see you, where you fit and what they think of you.

Remember - people gravitate towards others that they have a connection or an affinity with and in personal services, **people will always do business with people that they like.**

In a way, an experienced stylist is faced with an even larger problem; they have accumulated a wide variety of clients from different backgrounds built-up over a greater time-scale. Some of those will have become clients because of the influence of friends or family, others because of the trust that has developed over time. The only thing that all those accumulated clients have in common is their stylist, and that is where the link ends.

Remember, with nothing else defining them as a single target market, you will end up trying to be all things to all people.

If you wanted to develop a clientèle by design, rather than legacy, then you need to start afresh.

Client name	Where do they live?	Where do they go out?	What are their interests?	How did they become a client?	How regular is this client?
1. xxx	Xxxx	Xxxx	Xxxx	Xxxx	Xxxx
2. xxx					
3. xxx					
4. xxx					

2.05

Your business rules:

1.

You cannot be all things to all people

Be focused and make sure that your 'bread & butter' core services are of a consistent quality that you and your team can deliver every day without over-running and keeping clients waiting.

2.

Your clients are not your friends, but you may have friends that are also your clients

They say that there are no friendships in business.

For small, independent salon owners it is the hardest thing to come to terms with, let alone put into practice!

3.

Your business and ongoing success is based upon 80% communication and 20% technical ability

How shocking but it's true sadly!

You thought that your technical abilities were the reasons why people came to you in the first place. True, that was the reason, but when you got in to the routines of "same old thing – time after time," it was your communication and support that kept them coming back!

4.

Do not gossip or allow any of the staff to gossip!

If in doubt refer back to number 2

5.

Be the same with everyone

Your approach with all of your clients and the staff needs to be the same. Do not be false or make promises that you never keep. People like routines, (it is a natural fact of human nature) So when they get used to your personality and 'modus operandi' stick with it and they will stick with you.

The clients that go to stylists who have constant mood swings and tempers only do it to be entertained, that's not a good foundation for any business!

2.06

26

If you have been following the theme throughout this chapter, then you will have been spending a lot of time thinking about how you can meet the needs and expectations of your clients. This broad evaluation has made you look outwardly at the marketplace in which your business exists.

Now, in order to complete that process, you need a time of reflection and the simplest way of doing this would be through some form of self-analysis.

Strengths, weaknesses, opportunities & threats

SWOT analysis provides a systematic way for taking a snapshot of your current business attributes and will help you to create a plan of action.

SWOT relates to:

▶ *Strengths*

▶ *Weaknesses*

▶ *Opportunities*

▶ *Threats*

The analysis is carried out by taking an honest, *inward* look at your own strengths and then from this, identifying the opportunities that are available to you. Then by looking at your weaknesses, you will be able to consider the threats that present themselves *in light* of those factors.

Therefore, by doing a SWOT analysis you will be able to develop a plan of action and be able to move forwards. The process is designed to make you think about your business in a new way and therefore open your mind to what you can realistically achieve.

In simple terms, it focuses your mind on the important things that will affect your business in both positive and negative ways. It then identifies the things that you need to be doing in order to turn those negatives into positives.

You can create your long-term plans and plot the series of milestones or short-term objectives that will achieve the long-term aims.

Take a large sheet of paper and divide it into four with headings as shown below:

Do not worry at the length of any list at this stage, but try to prioritise the lists, so the strongest and weakest points are nearer to the top.

Strengths	Weaknesses
Opportunities	Threats

1.

Strengths	Weaknesses
Opportunities	Threats

2.

2.08   2.09

You need to focus upon your strengths first. Write down the things that from a business point of view make your business different and stand out from your competitors. These could relate to skills or training that your staff have had, or services and treatments that you provide that your competitors do not. It could even relate to location and *'footfall'*, or specific pricing advantages; such as, low rentals or bulk buying discounts.

After completing the business strengths, you should now focus upon the weaknesses and write them in under the heading. These could be things like lack of public visibility, say due to location or no window frontage. It could be linked to poor salon access which could deter potential clients from entering, i.e. being above or below other premises. It could relate to staff inexperience or lack of knowledge.

Moving on to the opportunities section, look back at your strengths and start to think about the unique opportunities that you have because of your strengths.

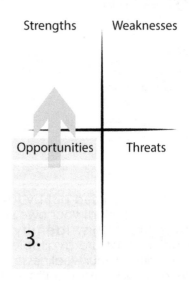

2.10

For example, your list may have identified the following strengths and therefore these opportunities might apply.

Example strengths

Strengths	Opportunities
Prominent busy location	Good opportunities to attract new custom from window display/promotion and special offers.
Regular staff training	Staff can promote new services, styles or products.
Good reputation	Provide an incentive to your clients to "Introduce a friend" and get others to develop your brand and marketing.
Unique product distribution	Prevents you having to compete on price against other salons selling the same or similar ranges. 2.11

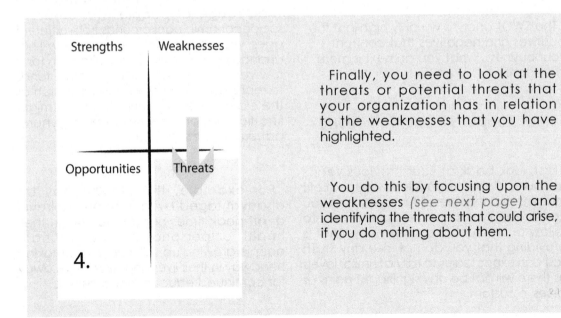

Finally, you need to look at the threats or potential threats that your organization has in relation to the weaknesses that you have highlighted.

You do this by focusing upon the weaknesses *(see next page)* and identifying the threats that could arise, if you do nothing about them.

2.12

Example weaknesses

Weaknesses	Threats
Poor salon frontage	Potential clients do not know that you are there and you lose business.
Salon situated on upper floors	Potential clients will be reluctant to walk up into a salon without knowing what to expect and again you lose business.
Poor staff technical skills	Potential clients could have expectations above and beyond your staff's capabilities, so that when they attend they are unhappy with the service they receive and give your salon a bad reputation.
Poor technical knowledge	Staff will not be able to explain the processes or products during consultation and things may go wrong during the technical services. This could give the salon a bad reputation and even lead to claims or legal action against the salon.

2.13

What next?

The SWOT analysis will only highlight the positives and negatives that confront your business, what you do next is more important.

What happens if you do nothing?

First, look back at your previous year's accounts. If you are satisfied with the profit margins and the overall turnover, then you can probably expect the current year to follow on in much the same way. That is providing that you do not lose any staff; you can expect sales to rally at similar levels as there will not be any significant gains or losses in custom.

If your clientèle is represented by a wide range of people with different socioeconomic backgrounds from different ages, you will find that your income will not change dramatically in any direction for a few years. However, if your clientèle tends to represent a particular grouping such as the elderly or very young, then you might find fluctuations in sales due to general patterns affecting them.

For example, the elderly may be disadvantaged by lack of public travel at off-peak times or changes within their health or personal income. Younger people growing up will want to be making headway in their lives and may move away for continued education or jobs, etc.

If you do nothing, you might get by for a couple of years, but remember, your staff may be looking to better themselves and could be looking to moving to one of your competitors! If you do not build-in any renewal into your plans, you will inevitably lose business, or *lose* your business!

What should I be doing?

The SWOT analysis is only the start; it is a mechanism for identifying the areas that you should be focusing upon and helps you to prioritize the work ahead. In completing the analysis you looked at your strengths and weaknesses first, this enabled you to identify the opportunities that were available to you and realized the threats that oppose your future success.

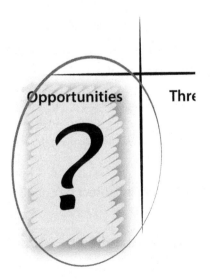

Get *SMART*

Look back at the opportunities that you have listed. Is your business moving towards any of those goals, if it is, have you set any time-scales to your plans? What about those threats, how long will the business continue before the threats have a severe impact upon your long-term security and success?

The simplest way of defining your business targets would be to use *SMART objectives.*

▸ Any objective that follows this is more likely to succeed because it is clear or **specific** so you know exactly what you need to achieve.

▸ You can tell when you achieve it because the completion is **measurable**.

▸ A SMART objective is likely to happen because it is an event that is **achievable**.

▸ Before setting a SMART objective, relevant factors such as the resources and time, should be taken into account to ensure that it is **realistic**.

▸ Finally, the **timescale** element provides a deadline that helps people focus on the tasks required to achieve the objective and stops people postponing the task's completion.

2.14

Example of SMART objectives

SMART elements	How they work in SMART objectives
Specific	The objective states that the business would like to **increase the amount of new customers** rather than something set in general terms such as increase profits.
Measurable	The objective states that the business would like to increase the clientèle **by 3 percent** This provides something measurable to show when the objective has been achieved.
Achievable	The planning stage should account for assessing whether **the objective is achievable.**
Realistic	The planning stage should account for assessing whether **the objective is realistic** in view of staffing, timing and other business resources.
Time bound	The objective must be achieved **within a 12 month timeframe** in order to be deemed as successful.

2.15

The forces acting upon a salon or spa business

The renowned educator and business guru *Michael E Porter*[1] identified five forces that act upon any business, and these are the ones that you have to address in order to survive:

▶ The power of *competitors*

▶ The power of *buyers* in the market

▶ The power of *suppliers* to the business

▶ The threats posed by *potential entrants*

▶ The threats posed by *substitute products*

2.16

If we look at each of these in relation to hairdressing, it might help to assess the scale of those forces and the potential impact upon your business.

The 5 Forces	What does it relate to?	What do you need to consider?
Competitors	The other salons in your locality that are attempting to win over your clients	➤ What do you know about your competitors? ➤ What is their public reputation like? ➤ What skills or specialist services does their staff possess? ➤ Which members of staff are the most popular and busiest?
Buyers	Your salon's customers Other salon's customers	➤ What keeps your clients coming back? ➤ What do they expect when they visit your salon? ➤ How do you stop them from going elsewhere? ➤ What do they buy from you? ➤ What do they buy from your competitors? ➤ What do you need to do to attract them to your salon?

2.17a

The 5 Forces	What does it relate to?	What do you need to consider?
Suppliers	The manufacturers and wholesalers that supply you with products	➤ Which of your competitors are they supplying with the same products? ➤ Do you have any buying advantages over your competitors? ➤ Do you have any distribution or exclusivity advantages? ➤ What are the chances of your competitors being able to gain the distribution advantages? ➤ How much support do you get from them?
Potential entrants	New salons opening in your area	➤ Is any of your staff looking to open their own business? ➤ Where will they be opening? ➤ Will they try to poach any friends or colleagues away from your business? ➤ What level of impact will it have on your business?
Substitute products	Competing products offering the same features and benefits possibly in a supermarket or store	➤ Do they provide similar benefits at a cheaper price? ➤ Are their products supported by better advertising? ➤ Are they easier to shop? ➤ Do they achieve better results than your products? ➤ Are they easier to use from a customer's point of view?

2.17b

You need to address each of these questions so that you can evaluate the *true* level of the threats that exist to the ongoing success of your business.

Target markets

Whilst working through this chapter, you should start to see a common thread occurring, and this should be flagging up the importance of knowing and understanding your target market.

When you started out in hairdressing, your initial success was attributable to two things, and this inspired you to go into business in the first place.

These two skills relate to your own:

▶ Personality

▶ Technical ability

These two personal attributes are still important, but only affect you and your clients; it has nothing to do with developing an ongoing successful business or a salon team. (It is one of the main reasons why mobile hairdressers work alone; their business relies solely upon their skills, and they have total control over their destiny.)

The skills that you need to apply go beyond this. You have to manage the personalities and technical skills of others; this is far harder to do, particularly when you are dealing with creative people and artistic temperaments!

However, you cannot be successful without them; you need their input as this has a direct impact on your *bottom line.*

Quite simply, you need the mix of clients that your staff contribute. They might not be the clients that you would choose, or have any affinity with, but they will make your business work.

Therefore, your target market is directly related to the staff that work for you and this should have a huge bearing on how you find and employ your staff. Many salons make the mistake of pinning their recruitment policy on the *'friends of friends'* network, and this will create a difficult business to manage. Finding the right people can be difficult, and many smaller businesses throw caution to the wind because they have immense problems attracting and keeping the right type of staff.

Never lose sight of the people that you want to attract and keep as clients. Map out the central *core* of your target market for your salon and extend this to encompass the *'wild and woolly'* periphery that is still with you today. (But might be gone tomorrow!) Then find staff that will help you to develop this *nucleus* as this is the only sure way of making your business success by design, rather than coincidence.

Make allowances for the staff losses and their replacements that happen along the way, but stick to the plan, do not deviate from your salon's business focus.

The following illustrations show the variety of customer groups that can be targeted. Each one provides a central core of typical clients and a periphery of similar types who could also be part of the representative group.

2.18

1. Affluent achievers

These are some of the most financially successful people; they live in wealthy, high status rural, semi-rural and suburban areas. Middle-aged or older people, the 'Baby-Boomer' generation, predominate with many wealthy and retired.

Some neighborhoods contain large numbers of 'well-off' families with school-age children, particularly the more suburban locations.

These people live in large houses, (usually detached) with four or more bedrooms. Some will own homes worth many millions. Typically, others live in homes that are significantly more expensive than the average for their locality.

▸ 10% will own a second property

▸ A high proportion are very well educated and employed in managerial and professional occupations

▸ Many own their own businesses

▸ Incomes are (generally) well above average

▸ Many can afford to spend freely and frequently and have also built up savings and investments

These people at the top of the social ladder and are usually confident with new technology and managing their finances,. They are healthy, wealthy and confident consumers.

2.19

2. Rising prosperity

These are (generally) younger, well-educated, prosperous people living in our major towns and cities, busily moving up the career ladder. Most are singles or couples, some yet to start a family, others with younger children.

Most live in converted or modern flats, with a significant proportion of these being recently built executive city flats. Others will live in terraced town houses and are buying their homes, whilst some will be renting.

While many have good incomes, not all might yet have had time to convert these into substantial savings or investments.

▶ They are likely to be financially confident, managing their money and choosing the provider of their financial, or other, services

▶ They are the internet generation, 'early adopters' most likely to use smartphones and frequently use the internet and new technology

▶ These people have a cosmopolitan outlook and enjoy their urban lifestyle

▶ They like to eat out in restaurants, go to the theatre and cinema and make the most of the culture and nightlife of the big city

COMFORTABLE COMMUNITIES

Countryside communities
Comfortable seniors
Successful suburbs

Steady neighbourhoods

2.20

3. Comfortable communities

This category contains much of middle-of-the-road in the suburbs, smaller towns or the countryside. Represented by all life-stages, many are within stable family groups and 'empty nesters,' are typical in suburban or semi-rural locations.

There are also the comfortably off pensioners, living in retirement areas around the coast or the countryside and sometimes younger couples just starting out on their lives together. Most people are comfortably off. They may not be very wealthy, but they have few major financial worries.

▶ People *(generally)* own their homes

▶ Most houses are semi-detached or detached, and a typical average value for the region

▶ Incomes are about average; although some will earn more, the younger people a bit less

▶ Those better established might have built up a degree of savings or investments

▶ Employment is in a mix of professional and managerial, clerical and skilled occupations

▶ Educational qualifications tend to be in line with the national average

2.21

4. Financially stretched

Housing tends to be terraced or semi-detached, there is a mix of lower value owner-occupied housing and homes rented from councils or housing associations. This includes social housing developments specifically for the elderly.

This category also includes student term-time areas. There tend to be fewer traditional married couples than usual and higher proportions of single parents. (Single, separated and divorced people.)

Incomes tend to be well below average, although some will have reasonably well-paid jobs.

▶ People tend to work in lower-paid administrative, clerical, semi-skilled and manual jobs

▶ Apprenticeships and 'O' levels are more likely to be the standard educational qualifications

▶ Unemployment is above average as are the proportions of people claiming other benefits

▶ People are less likely to engage with financial services

▶ Fewer people are likely to have a credit card, investments, a pension scheme, or much savings

▶ Some are likely to have been refused credit

▶ Some will be having difficulties with debt

▶ These people are less likely than average to use new technology or to shop online, or research using the internet, although will use the internet socially

Overall, while many people in this financially stretched category are just getting by with modest lifestyles, a significant minority are experiencing some degree of financial pressure.

housing that is owner-occupied is of low value. Where values are influenced by higher urban property prices these are still lower value relative to the location.

5. Urban adversity

2.22

This category contains the most deprived areas of large and small towns and cities. Household incomes are low, nearly always below national averages. The level of people having difficulties with debt or having been refused credit approaches double the national average. The numbers claiming benefits are well above the national averages. Levels of qualifications are low, and those in work are likely to be in semi-skilled or unskilled employment.

The housing is a mix of low-rise estates, with terraced and semi-detached houses, and purpose built flats, including high-rise blocks. The relatively small proportion of

▶ Over half of the housing is rented from the local council or a housing association

▶ Properties tend to be small, and there may be overcrowding

▶ There is some private renting

▶ There are a large number of single adult households

▶ Many single pensioners, lone parents, separated and divorced people

▶ They often (relatively) have higher levels of health problems

These are the people who are finding life the hardest and experiencing the most difficult social and financial conditions.

3

THE SALON & SUPPLIER RELATIONSHIP

The salon & supplier relationship

The initial approach

In life, we often wonder why things happen and more often than not we accept them as routine occurrences or coincidences.

Well, to a certain extent that is true, but it does not cover every eventuality. In reality, things happen for a reason and in a situation where a manufacturer's sales representative walks into your salon, they have turned up because they have targeted you as a new potential account.

Before thinking about the relationship between you and your supplier, pause for a moment to consider this adage. *"Which came first, the chicken or the egg?"* In being asked so many times, by so many people it still doesn't have any single answer that satisfies everyone.

Who controls the salon & supplier relationship?

Most salon owners are in awe of their product suppliers; they feel small and insignificant in relation to the multi-national manufacturers. If that is true, why should they knock on your door looking for business?

Take a few moments to consider the following:

▶ Why have we allowed the manufacturer to dictate their terms for so long?

▶ When did they take control?

▶ Should we expect to be managed by suppliers in similar ways that we manage our clients?

▶ Are we powerless in the supplier - customer relationship?

The majority of salons share these thoughts and most view manufacturers as being responsible for 'flooding' the market with products via the Internet, the High Street stores and supermarkets. Then after doing this they expect the salons to buy their products in situations where they cannot compete on a *like for like* basis.

This particular situation has provoked a lot of bad feelings and mistrust and has fueled many networking discussion threads. So now, more than ever before, the manufacturers' agents and representatives work very hard to get appointments with the salon owners and in doing so, try to rectify those wrongs and re-build the professional relationships.

On the surface, the salon and manufacturer relationship seems very simple and straightforward, but with whom are we getting involved?

*Salon & supplier relationships - **who are we dealing with?***

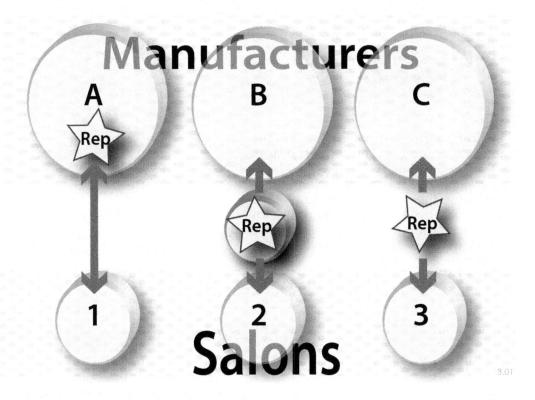

3.01

Situation A+1	The manufacturer *employs* sales representatives and each one makes a connection directly with the salon on behalf of their employer.
Situation B+2	A manufacturer links with a distributor, in this case a wholesaler. The sales representative is employed by the *wholesaler* and will be trained by the manufacturer so that they can have expert knowledge of their particular product ranges.
Situation C+3	A *self-employed* representative acts on behalf of the manufacturer and works independently to make connections with salons after receiving product training and other support

3.02

In most cases, the manufacturer initiates the salon contact at the request of their distributor or supplier. A call will normally occur when they feel that the salon is ready to increase their commitment to product ranges and other retail products. It may also occur when the sales representative or distributor sees that purchases are tailing off, or they feel that they may be losing an account.

Note: When salons make late payments on their account, or when trading patterns change dramatically, it will be flag-up internally to the manufacturer and will be acted upon very quickly.

At times when trading patterns change for the worse, the manufacturer will take measures to attempt some damage limitation in order to keep the account *alive on their books* and still actively trading.

The bigger picture

Many salons do not see themselves as being part of an overall selling and marketing machine. Most salons are small independent firms and (quite rightly) only concerned about things that affect them. However, from the manufacturer's point of view, they are an integral part of the

sales chain; the essential stewards and advocates of their business. They are the customer-facing element of the selling process and can either enhance their products' reputation or *kill it!*

Thinking on from this, what are the feelings that you experience when a sales representative turns up in your reception asking to speak to the owner or manager?

▶ **Do you feel particularly happy about the situation, or are you inconvenienced or even intimidated by the intrusion?**

The majority of busy salons find that any unsolicited impromptu sales calls as an inconvenience and would think along the lines of:

▶ **Why have they turned up now?**

▶ **Why are they wasting my time?**

Quite simply, they are just opportunists who are looking for any angle to make contact with you. Remember, they already know about their products ranges that you use and even the ones bought indirectly through a 3rd party supplier. Therefore under the guise of a courtesy call, they are preparing some sales patter to launch, promote and convert your salon to their rationale.

One of the most important factors of any product's sales success is linked to knowing who the potential customers are and how much they are willing to spend. This key information is vitally important to the manufacturer, and they have the skills and resources to research their salon prospects and grade them accordingly. The grading system A, B, C, etc. provides a prioritized list that focuses the sales team's attention and provides a pecking order or preference group. Quite often, this will be based on competitor information, and the profile of the product ranges that a salon already uses. Alternatively, it can be based upon the numbers of hairstylists that work in a salon, as this is a good indicator of a salon's potential sales/turnover.

For example, *A salon with five stylists all fully booked working five days a week could be seeing upwards of two hundred clients each week. So if you multiply this by the average hourly income or service, and you start to see quite an impressive turnover?*

Any salon chain will be considered a *Grade A* target and will be on the top of any manufacturer's priority list. These businesses are harder to convert, but will always provide the highest returns.

However, the majority of salons are not large companies, **they are smaller independents employing on average as little as five staff in total.** Therefore, any salon employing **five or more stylists** will also rank very highly on a grading system and can expect to attract many unsolicited callers.

Working along these lines, the larger manufacturer will be targeting the larger salons first. Then they will work down their lists to the lower grades until they reach the point where the target is considered non-viable. For this reason, some smaller enterprises would be better off considering links with smaller suppliers, perhaps with a more bespoke, or niche product ranges.

It is a numbers game, - what will be the salon's turnover during the year? Then taking the gross figure, how much will be allocated to the purchases of consumables? What potential is there to increase sales, say by retailing; encouraging the clients to *lock-in* to particular product ranges.

What would stimulate or entice you to respond to a sales representative's spiel? What sort of incentives will encourage you to spend more?

Gone fishing....

Unsolicited visits by sales representatives are normally geographically focused, so after some initial research, the manufacturer will field a sales person or team, into an area on a fact-finding mission.

Sales reps will often make an accompanied visit to the salon and will introduce their area field technician in a two-pronged approach. It provides an alternative point of contact who can immediately answer any technical questions as well as being part of the sales support. These trainers/educators play a key role in bridging that the gap between education and sales and normally have a practical salon background, making them the ideal recruit.

Manufacturers know that training/ education is the *key* to unlocking doors, and they use it as a method of getting a foothold in the salon. The field technician's salon background is invaluable and provides an *insider's* approach to sales opportunities, and creates a direct relationship with the decision makers.

In any event, the main aim of the sales team is to find a way of booking a future appointment.

Remember when someone makes eye contact with someone else, it is very difficult (unless they are naturally rude) to ignore.

How will they approach me?

Their first task is to get past the receptionist and be able to engage you in some exchange of words. On entering the salon, they will be quickly trying to find out who the decision maker is and whether they are available. The usual stock answer from the receptionist gives the *game away* by saying.

"I'm afraid he/she is busy with a client at the moment......"

Gotcha! It will immediately alert the reps to the fact that the decision maker is there, and now all they have to do is look around casually to see who has noticed their entrance. **From a salon psychology point of view, the salon owner/manager will always try to make eye contact with every visitor to the salon.** They do this partly because of their professional experience, but also because they have a vested interest in all business activity. The other stylists tend to carry on talking with their clients whilst doing their hair and take very little notice of people that they do not know or recognize.

Therefore, in this situation the salon owner or manager is quickly and easily revealed and the next task for the representative is to make eye contact.

A foot in the door!

At the point where the potential target has now been identified, the next step is to engage them in some form of verbal exchange and conversation is always the starting point of any negotiations. It does not matter how good you are communicating with clients; people in sales know that they only have moments to capture and focus your attention.

At this point, many working salon managers make the mistake of responding naturally to their *opening gambit*.

"How's business?"

"How are you finding your retail sales are doing?"

Alternatively, in a more focused approach with a definite hook.

"I wonder if you might find some time for me to talk about and present our rewards program?"

During all this time, they are *fishing* for a way in; an opportunity to get your time and attention as the salon owner or manager. Maybe you consider this slightly underhand but they are only doing their job and offering you a business opportunity.

Remember, you can always say no thank you, they are sales people and trained to accept (or unaffected by) rejection. They work on averages and percentages i.e. the number of cold call visits made in one day divided by the number of follow-ups or re-visit appointments that they make.

The manufacturer & the distributor

As we have already seen in the previous illustration, (3.01) a manufacturer may use a local wholesaler as their intermediary. In this scenario, the manufacturer works very closely with all the distributors in the area. (Remember, it is in their interest to stay in good favor as they don't want to lose their distribution business within the area.)

The goal of any manufacturer is twofold:

1. Have as much exposure and coverage in an area

2. Supply any number of outlets within that area with their product ranges

It is quite easy to see the direct links between both statements, but when saturation point is reached, the coverage goes beyond the professional outlets and enters into the retail stores too.

It is common knowledge within the professional industry that the larger manufacturers own many different brands, and each marketed as separate product lines, aimed at different markets with different types of customer.

We also know that large manufacturers produce products for both the professional market, as well as the public. The only difference between them being the pricing policy, packaging and formulations. Historically, it is this diversification that has bruised the reputation of professional supplier market.

Deception

New products are normally launched to the professional market first. It gives salons some exclusivity for a while, but they often end up being used as guinea pigs in the longer term. Whilst the salons build new a new customer base for the products over the first year or so, the manufacturers will produce their *thinly disguised* cheaper copies for the retail stores and supermarkets. The technology used in developing the original, professional product is now reused and repurposed for the ready, willing and waiting customers.

Good intentions & positive impressions

What are their intentions when targeting your business? Quite simply, it is to increase their share of the market in your salon if you are already using and promoting their products, or to switch you over to their products if you are a *holdout*.

Remember, they already have a picture of how busy you are and an idea of your annual sales and retail turnover. (Also, where you 'fit in' to the existing marketplace, i.e. in relation to your peers and competitors). Therefore, they now need to start to build a relationship. How do they do this, by offering you an incentive!

One of the main analytical tools for any business is the identification of needs - **needs analysis**. If you find out what people need, then you only have to find ways to provide or deliver it at the time that suits them and at a price they are willing to pay.

Remember, their sources can be distributors and suppliers, but in most situations, the information will come from you or your staff. They need a foot-in-the-door, and the best way to do this is by apparently giving you something.

Free samples, client gifts or staff development; these are most popular, tried and tested things that we need and will benefit our business. "When I was involved in sales and education, I liked doing my research and building relationships with the salon team and owner. I knew that having that having that opportunity to talk with the team was very important to any potential sales."

The sales appointment & salon visit

After the initial contact, a *courtship* begins. The rep's first formal meeting is a fact-finding mission to evaluate the salon account potential.

Preparation

The first meeting is a 'scene setter' for the representative, as it provides the only opportunity to find out more about you!

Until this point, the majority of what the supplier thinks that they know about you is speculative.

You have permitted them to make an appointment with you, and now it is their chance to see if the hearsay and gossip, conjecture and assumptions, match up to the reality.

You can expect them to prepare their pitch well and they will have a range of things that they will want to present to you.

They hope to find out the following:

➤ Your particular likes and dislikes within salon products

➤ The size of your existing budget and annual spend on product resources

➤ Your salon's target market *(see chapter 2)*

➤ The demographic profile of your regular clients   *(see chapter 2)*

➤ The products that could be introduced to fill gaps in existing ranges

➤ Opportunities to replace existing, competing ranges with their own products

➤ Any problems that you have with competing suppliers or their products

3.06

Many small salon managers are unprepared for their business to be 'put under the microscope.' They can often feel intimidated and will start to make things up as they go along, or worse; overstate their trading position and try to *brag and boast* their way through it.

Either approach is wrong and can be a potentially, very costly mistake. An inexperienced manager can be easily cornered and end up accepting a deal just because they got talked into it.

So, what as a salon owner should you be expecting and what is the manufacturer hoping to achieve?

Remember, it 'works' both ways and can be very beneficial for all parties, providing that a clear mutual respect exists from the outset.

Take the time to think about the meeting and through the sorts of questions that you need to ask and the things that you would like to see.

From the manufacturers' point of view, they have reached *first base* they have a meeting, and this gives them a platform from which they can build their relationships. It provides an opportunity to present their products and to discuss all the support that comes from a more committed business relationship.

Things you should ask	Things you could see
➤ How would a newly introduced range be supported if it were taken on?	➤ Examples of the ranges under discussion and the size options available
➤ Is there any educational support / how would that be delivered?	➤ Samples of the ranges that could be used during testing with clients
➤ How would a manufacturer handle resistance amongst staff to embed new product ranges?	➤ Point of sale material, display material advertising, public awareness campaigns - (e.g. radio, TV, Internet)
➤ What are the benefits to the salon for using a new range(s)	➤ Brochures, client information, leaflets, Take-ones,
➤ Costs, discounts, buying levels, key account benefits	➤ Price lists and introductory deals
➤ Product target market / client demographics	➤ Themed or seasonal gifts that may be accompanying a product launch
➤ Customer benefits of selecting one range over another	➤ Profiles of the salons who are already using their products
➤ Exclusivity, who else will be distributing the same (competing) products within a geographical area	➤ Testimonials from other salons that are already using the products
➤ Terms of sale / payments / credit arrangements	➤ Plans for future advertising campaigns and ongoing support

3.07

Remember, they have huge resources, a well-educated team of sales representatives, advisors and field technicians, all at their disposal. Their end aim is quite simple, and that is to expand existing accounts, open new ones and convert hold-outs to use their product options.

As prospective purchasers, you should be thinking about the quality, pricing, packaging and suitability of the products on offer and how this will work with your existing clientèle.

It is pointless to consider buying a range just because you like it; you have to put yourself in your client's position and see how the benefits will help them.

For example. There is little point considering a new permanent color range that is guaranteed to cover gray hair 100% if the majority of your clientèle is under thirty. Similarly, a 'funky' niche packaged styling product range, promoted by a *Teen-Idol* pop group, will be incongruous in young professionals' bathrooms.

....

Remember, it is all about your clients' needs and what will work best for the salon, for the business and what your staff will welcome and be able to sell.

....

Remember, the manufacturer considers all of these factors, but for them, it is all about 'their account' and future sales.

Pause for thought...

We, as professionals know that the majority of our clients are totally unaware of the manufacturer names that sit behind all of those global brands. As an interesting exercise, it would be useful to recap now, on just how big our industry is.

What a huge role we play in supporting and advocating these companies, yet how small are we in comparison, as individual salons.

Without looking at any one manufacturer with preference or bias, I would like to share some information before we move on. It is especially relevant when thinking about which manufacturer to work with and where you see mutual benefits.

OK. If you have done your homework, think about the following brand names:

When you think of a manufacturer what other brands do you associate with them?

Manufacturer	Related Brands
L'Oreal	➤ Matrix ➤ Redken ➤ Pureology ➤ Kerastase ➤ Garnier
Estee Lauder	➤ Aveda ➤ Bumble & Bumble
KAO	➤ Goldwell ➤ KMS California ➤ John Freida ➤ Molton Brown
Proctor & Gamble	➤ Wella ➤ Vidal Sassoon ➤ Aussie ➤ Sebastian ➤ System Professional ➤ Nice & Easy
ISO	➤ Joico ➤ ISO
Unilever	➤ TIGI ➤ Bed Head

3.08

How many brands did you recognize and did you know that they were made by only a few manufacturers?

We know that they produce professional product ranges, but they still sell competing ranges to the supermarkets too. How do your clients distinguish between them when they only recognize the manufacturer's names?

How will you educate your clients and distinguish the differences between the benefits of professional and shop bought products?

How will you answer the questions that your clients will have in relation to the two types of products?

Think about how it will benefit **you** and **your team**, as you are not (at this point) looking to place an order (nor would they expect you to) as this is the first date.

During the meeting focus your interests on the facts; show just enough interest to make them keen to come back and prepared to offer you a better deal.

You may well decide that you need to see more than one representative and the illustration overleaf might help you to consider your options. If you are considering looking at more than one brand or product range, be honest, keep your options open and avoid *closing* the doors.

Remember, the first meeting is like a two-way interview - you to them and them to you. They will feel that it has been a success if they leave you wanting more time to think - but wanting to book another appointment as well.

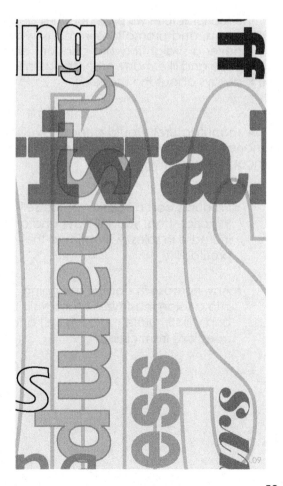

Deals, discounts & key accounts

OK, you have had the time to think about the questions that you need to ask, you have an idea of what you and your team want. The manufacturer's representative will certainly have considered what they need to do in order to make a deal happen and what they can offer the salon.

When is a deal a deal?

The manufacturer will package their deals, discounts, and promotions in many ways, it is never a straightforward discount on a set price and like many other things in life, it is always about the money.

A manufacturer would rather have the money and provide more products as an incentive because:

▸ Products cost a fraction of the selling price (that you will pay) and any increase in sales, will optimize their profitability

▸ Any increase in stock levels going into a salon maximizes brand visibility and will stimulate more interest and questions from clients.

3.10

Typically, they could offer three for two as a retail incentive, and this is very popular, but only useful if the salon staff is geared to retailing products.

With any introduction of new products, it is essential that there is some form of training and product knowledge support. Getting the team to *buy* into the concept is as important to the manufacturer as it is for you.

Your team members need to learn about the products that they are recommending and using. Otherwise, they will be reluctant in trying them in the first place.

Products are not wallpaper!

They are not just pretty items used to cheer up a *dingy* corner; they have far more important purposes. Retail displays are an expensive investment for the salon and stock resting on shelves is an expensive cost. Products provide a useful, additional input to the salons income, and many salons look to achieve a significant proportion of their overall annual turnover through their retail sales.

There are hidden benefits to the purposes of retailing that you may not have thought about. The promotional displays play an integral part in supporting the salon's image. The salon only purchases products for use and resale that reflect the quality of services being offered.

The sale of retail products enables the clients to gain an extension of the salon experience, in the products that they take home.

*As a salon, let us assume that you were looking to add working stock and retail products to your salon. You have had the first meeting and received the **sales pitch** now you want to know what's on offer, what it's going to cost, what support you can expect to get.*

If this scenario *chimes* with your salon, then you need to be thinking about what you expect to gain.

Question. *What is your expectation from introducing more of these products?*

Answer. *To increase sales by making them available to your clients through your salon team.*

If this is true, your staff will need to:

1. Support the product introduction

2. Learn about the features and benefits of the products

3. Talk about them (create a salon buzz) during consultation and services

Then any deal should include:

A. **Free samples** - *things you can use with or provide to your clients*

B. **Display material** - *Point of Sale, posters, charts, brochures, leaflets*

C. **In-salon education** - *a field technician/educator to spend a day in the salon, talking with clients, working on the salon floor, working with staff at the basin area and in the dispensary, offering clients complimentary treatments to help promote the products.*

I would also try to get some introductory product support deal from my rep; this could go along the lines of getting a certain amount of free product for the salon. For example, backwash shampoo and conditioner that matches the new range, but in retail sizes.

Things to consider:

- ☑ Number of stylists that you have

- ☑ How busy the stylists are

- ☑ The ratio of the services you offer (i.e. chemical to styling)

- ☑ Your stock holding levels

- ☑ Any incentives that you are going to offer your staff

- ☑ The method of promoting the products to your clients

3.11

The checklist above provides a quick overview of things to consider. Remember the stock has to work for you so it needs to be moving off the shelf at a steady rate so that you can pay your supplier within twenty-eight days.

Figuratively speaking...

If we consider an example of a deal that you have been offered by the manufacturer on shampoo.

SPECIAL OFFER!

Buy 10 get 12 - unit cost **5.00** including tax **20%**
Recommended retail price (MRRP) **10.00** including tax

Amount purchased	Unit cost price	Selling price	Total returns if sold		Gross profit
10	5.00	10.00	100.00		50.00

Amended potential return after adding a 10% stylist commission

Amount purchased	Unit cost price	Selling price	Total return	Commission	Gross profit
10	5.00	10.00	92.00	8.00	42.00

3.13

On paper, it looks OK and particularly as we have the two extra bottles that we can sell without any additional cost. So our 40.00 net profit increases to 48.00 (Ex-tax) on our 50.00 investment. But are we forgetting something? Yes, there needs to be some incentive for the stylists, so we need to factor in a commission say at 10%.

0.80 per bottle (Ex-tax) This is not a great deal, but over the ten it amounts to 8.00 and on 12 it returns 9.60. However, this will come off the projected 56.00 when the initial 12 bottles sell and this gives us a total of 46.40 as a return on our initial investment.

Example used for illustration only - tax within purchases and tax applied upon gross sales will differ.

57

In this scenario, the investment does seem worthwhile but only if all the products sell. It illustrates the importance of realistically working out what's best for you and your business beforehand. A deal is only a *deal* when it matches the size and scale of your business; i.e. staff numbers, number of outlets, client demographics, etc. For a smaller salon, I would recommend trying a mix of products on offer, so you get both shampoo and conditioner; maybe 6 of each rather than having to buy large amounts of one product type. Remember, if you overbuy, it is very hard to return or swap retail products to the manufacturer once delivered.

The Key Account

The term **key account** from a manufacturer or supplier point of view is a high profile salon (or salon chain) with a large budget for purchases. Many of these may have celebrity stylists and a high or prominent profile, some will be *household* names. However, regardless of location, status, and size, the manufacturers' key accounts are those that (relatively speaking) spend the more than their other accounts.

....

"I also think that having worked with distributors and in sales, they see every salon as a potential key account. They are aware of salon size and the scale of business being traded, but they are also committed to working with every salon and in helping them to maximize their potential."

....

A Key Account is a broad term; to some manufacturers it could be a salon, a chain or franchise, but it may be a college too. Educational establishments are a natural target for a manufacturer as there are many benefits in dealing with the educators.

*See table on the next page

The other type of key account is the one that involves the salon committing to a single manufacturer as a 'one stop shop.' In this scenario the salon purchases all of their hair coloring, perming and lightening products as well as treatments, conditioners and styling ranges.

From the manufacturer's point of view, having a salon that is totally reliant on them for all their products and ranges puts them in a very powerful position. On the other hand, it makes a salon vulnerable, because all of the salon's clients get used to the benefits from a particular brand. If the salon then changes its supplier or starts to introduce other competing ranges, the clients may look elsewhere for their products.

Sharp practice & sales tactics

The most effective sales strategy is made up from the simplest sequence of discussion threads, and you need to be aware of these 'traps' as they occur. If you bear in mind that the most effective way of selling anything is basing them upon someone's needs then, it will always follow these steps:

Colleges are a typical Key Account targets

What are the reasons?	Why does this happen?
They have large numbers of students who during their initial training will be getting used to specific products and ranges	People tend to stick with things that they know and will therefore leave education and prefer to continue using things with which they feel confident
Students do not have any preconceived ideas or knowledge about products	Hair stylists will always revert back to their initial training as being a starting point for their knowledge and understanding
Students are being taught by educators who have a breadth of knowledge and experience	People learn from those in which they have respect and have helped them in one-to-one situations
The staff are very receptive to presentations from industry suppliers	Teachers are easier to sell to than salon owners and managers because they are not spending their own money
Teaching staff use in-college training by manufacturers as:	➤ Easy options for lesson planning ➤ Exciting external visits by leading educators ➤ Ways to develop their own knowledge and continuing professional development

3.14

59

The manufacturer's representative will do the following:

☑ *Ask questions about your existing ranges*

These questions will identify the ranges that you already use and sell as retail to your clients. It provides them with a list of competing ranges that have direct links/similarities/benefits that can be matched to their alternatives.

☑ *Listen to pick up on areas where there are problems, issues or (ideally) dissatisfaction*

The rep will probe further on particular ranges where other salons have reported: difficulties/problems/negative feedback from clients

☑ *Expand on the areas where there are problems*

The rep will ask you about your specific problems with any of these products and the corrective measures, steps or action that you have taken. They will be particularly interested in areas that remain unresolved.

☑ *Provide solutions to your problem*s

After making the problem seem larger they will provide you with an alternative, that can be backed up by either a scientific principle (in theory will eliminates the problem) or by using another salon's testimony (ideally a competitor or a leading industry name - to make you really take notice)

☑ *Gain your instant commitment*

A direct question of when you want to take up their offer and in some holdout situations possibly 'swap-out' the problem range and replace it with their own.

3.15

How does the manufacturer open a new color account?

We can see the steps that a rep might take in moving towards 'closing a sale,' but how does this work in a real salon setting?

In most cases, the rep will look for signs of dissatisfaction. For example, hair color is a huge expense for a salon and an essential element for its success and profitability. When things are going well, the clients and staff are happy and everything is fine, however, this can change so quickly if a colorist starts to get issues with product's reliability or consistency. A similar state of 'blind-panic' occurs when the clients start to notice and report issues with their color, such as **build-up, banding or fading and durability.**

In nine out of ten cases when a stylist experiences poor or unsatisfactory results, the cause is due to application or lack of product knowledge, and this can provide a range of problems. Uneven deposit, color bands/banding, color fade, or poor coverage.

Nobody is perfect, but some mistakes border on incompetence: If we do not do a full consultation, keep good records, measure chemicals accurately, then the result can be a disaster. Imagine baking a cake and measuring the ingredients by eyesight alone, there is a strong likelihood that something will go wrong.

More often than not, when something goes wrong in a salon situation, it is not the fault of the hair stylist, there must be something wrong with the product!

This scenario provides the manufacturer's representative with the perfect solution, and the offer will come in exchanging your existing color stock on a *tube-for-tube swap.*

Now back this up with some educational support, and you are heading towards an annual four-figure commitment.

Don't take their word for it

When considering switching to a new color range always remember to investigate the manufacturer's claims before you buy! For example, the unit cost of a tube, bottle, applicator or canister might seem appealing but consider the manufacturer's instruction in relation to product sizing and mixing ratios.

Product A. Might be sold as 60 ml units and cost 10.00 with a mixing ratio of *1 : 1.5* with cream developer, in this instance you might get 2 applications per tube, which after salon costs are removed, may provide a profitable return.

Product B. Might be sold in 90 ml units still cost 10.00 but have a mixing ratio *2 : 1* in this instance you would only get 1 1/2 applications per tube and therefore it is more expensive and less profitable on a like for like basis.

In other scenarios a manufacturer may recommend that in order to improve coverage on gray hair you need to use a higher ratio of the color product say *1.5 : 1* or *3 : 1* - *this would make the service totally non-profitable!*

3.17

The offer - 'cutting a deal'

Remember, that quantities and product quality are very important, and the financial security of your business may depend on it.

How do you optimize your buying potential?

We have already looked at a variety of different scenario's relating to retail stock and product purchases supporting a variety of services.

We have also considered switching from one manufacturer to another by product swaps. Regardless of this you should never feel rushed or intimidated; these are big decisions with long-term implications. You cannot afford to make mistakes by agreeing to switch then expect to change your mind. It could prove very costly and very disruptive to the salon in a variety of different ways from demotivated staff or customer repeated sales.

"If you need more advice - why not join my professional group."

www.linkedin.com - *Professional Hairdressers Knowledge Network*

Think about your business, the on-going implementation of your business plan, your marketing strategy and ask yourself, does this offer meet your needs and requirements. How does this new proposal allow you to offer better customer service, whilst increasing your sales and profitability? Does the offer fit your existing business plan, or are you taking a gamble by venturing into the unknown?

Communication is everything, so never be afraid voice your concerns, if you are unsure, say no. You are exchanging information that is leading to a negotiated agreement for the future, so it has to be right. Can you afford it, are your aims based on sound financial forecasts or are they the desires of vanity; *just a wish list to keep up with the competition?*

The final decision is always yours, and it may be the answer to your long-term success. Remember that your good name is your reputation, and this can only be achieved by your repeated high standard of work. i.e. The quality of what you and your staff provide and the content of your services. It is this level of service that your clients are satisfied with and what makes them return on a regular basis. Your business is not just another *free* advertising location for some other company's corporate branding, and *you should never feel that your work is secondary to the products that you sell and use*.

You can only benefit if it raises the profile and profitability of your business. Never make the mistake of thinking that by trading *off the back* of a well-supported brand name will improve your hairstyling abilities, it will not, it is merely an extension of what you already do.

The salon & manufacturer relationship

A manufacturer's representative is not your friend!

I suppose that you thought that the *gossip* and 'idle chit-chat' in hairdressing are confined to the staff room, well, unbelievably, it takes place in the salon too! Sadly, it does not end there either; gossip occurs in wider spheres too, and some can be extremely damaging for your business.

The majority of hair salon businesses are micro-businesses where an owner or manager is responsible for just a handful of staff. Small need not be a negative aspect; in many ways, it is quite the reverse and is an ideal model for small business everywhere. However, we all have our weaknesses and in business, size can be a problem.

Always maintain a professional relationship with your supplier and never be drawn into discrediting your competitors, regardless of how much it would please you. The manufacturer's rep or agent is not your friend, so never be tempted to divulge anything that you would not want your competitors to find out!

Remember, these people know exactly how much you spend on consumables, and it only takes a simple calculation to work out that this is roughly 15% of your gross turnover. Your suppliers know a lot about you so if they start telling you gossip about your competitors, what are they saying to them, behind your back?

"Mutual trust and respect are such an important aspect of the professional relationship; it will not work without it. I found that building and developing relationships were 'key' to my success, particularly in doing in-salon education, for increasing sales and even 'switching' salons to new color lines."

"Honesty was always the best servant. I would always take the time to sit with a salon owner and sometimes work together to help get the staff 'on-board' or sometimes questioning their motives or decisions."

"A salon owner or the salon team does not want or need a flaky sales person; i.e. one who's only objective is to get more product into the salon. However, many try to attempt this strategy, but they always fail miserably in the longer term."

"As a field technician and educator working for and on behalf of the manufacturer, my sole aim was to create sales from a platform built on assistance and education."

"In order for this to work, I had to nurture the trust of both the salon owner and the team. In developing this type of relationship, I had to be good at 'reading' people and being able to communicate on many levels, conscientiously and with humility."

"There is no place for EGO when trying to develop these relationships, far too many educators go into a salon with an attitude and belief that they are better than those that they train. Not true, we have just been trained to share our knowledge and share the information we have been trained to deliver. When working in salons alongside the stylists and the owner, I might advise on hair color or be involved in consultations, but only in ways that will help the operator find the correct solutions."

"I share this with you as an example, a model for a relationship that works. It is all about good service, communication, listening and hearing, but above all professionalism. "

Regarding sales reps & field technicians

"The relationship between the sales representative and the salon is always different from the one built by the educator and the salon. In my experience, I was the facilitator; the one offering to give and support, rather than the one who was selling. You could say that our goals were the same, but the method was different, and that is why I can relate to the issues that many stylists have about retail and selling. I have some sympathy for those that struggle with this, but I cannot sit on the fence in this one, I believe that we are all in the business of sales and selling."

'Real' ongoing support

The salon owner wants a relationship that they can trust; they want to feel supported and need to feel that the specific attributes of their business that are unique to them are heard and clearly understood. This formula creates a working relationship and one that works on many levels, partly due to being respectful, but more importantly, by keeping the professional boundaries well defined. A true professional will never try to dictate terms, have a take it or leave it attitude, or jeopardize a bond for the sake of making a quick sale.

Salon hierarchy

We know that the reception is the key area in any salon, it is the hub, the *engine room* and normally a salon owner places a great deal of responsibility and autonomy in their receptionist. These people are formidable and warrant a great deal of respect and as a trade connection, if you get off to a *bad start* with them, it is *downhill* all the way.

As external contacts, we know that we cannot create a workaround for a receptionist. If someone were to try and sidestep, or sideline them, it's virtually game over. Therefore, in thinking about their role and what they can command, you would be missing out if you were not using them to 'bat-off' unwanted, unsolicited or improper business communications. The solution is simple; brief your receptionist well, and they will act as your front line business manager. We know that they hold the key to your appointment schedule, and we will have to fit in with whatever they offer.

The receptionist is normally responsible for optimizing the retail display, replenishing the products and recording the sales. Therefore, they have a very good working knowledge and insight into what products are selling, what ones need help, or are just not moving. Sales reps tend to target them for information particularly, as they have a cross-salon overview of retail products and more importantly, which stylists are remembering to recommend products to their clients and those that are not. The owner/manager will have a figurative record of the same information but may not want to focus upon specific technicians. Again, for the manufacturer, this is useful feedback as it allows the educator to work more closely with those that are flagged up as needing more help or one-to-one assistance.

Didn't we do well?

Receptionists also get a lot of client feedback, and this can be very useful to all parties. (If we can get this information from the receptionist, we have a good opportunity to anticipate the salon's needs) Salon information gives us a *heads-up* in a business meeting and focuses the management's attention on issues before they become a problem.

Great collaboration, simple strategy, it works every time.

Arranging future rep's visits

We know that the receptionist plays a vital role in the smooth running of the salon and that they are the first point of contact for any enquiries or appointments.

Business meetings need to be booked well in advance, and all representatives know that the clients *(naturally)* tend to take a preference. Therefore, a sales rep will always book their next call before they leave the salon and give an indication of how long it will take.

Appointments need to be arranged at mutually agreeable times and provide enough time for covering all the aspects thoroughly. Do not fall into the trap of thinking that when you have done the major *'intro' deal* that future meetings can be covered in five minutes. They will always take a lot longer.

Your supplier will be keen to show you a new offer or deal on each visit, some will interest you; others will not. Keep abreast of what is happening in the trade and consumer press, and you will get an insight of what is coming up and be prepared to talk about it. Ignorance will not help and as an active member within the industry; you have a duty to keep on top of all the developments in your specialist field.

Remember, you might not owe this allegiance to your supplier, but you do owe it to your clients.

Remember, you want your clients to be talking about you and what you do, to their friends and families at home. Therefore, you need to be doing your homework beforehand, so they have got something to discuss.

At each meeting have an agenda and be working towards the next marker for growth or success. Set your targets and do your best to meet them, if the targets prove too high, no problem, learn from it this month and adjust your expectations for next.

Remember to have your staff meetings prior to any rep's visit. Gather their feedback and record any questions that you need to ask on individual's behalf. If further educational visits are planned or required, find out what the team wants to see, what do they need to know? Do you need to arrange models for the technician and if so, what technical tasks and services do you want to see?

Discuss the promotional support, poster campaigns, and in-salon displays.

▶ Are they working, do your team bring them to their client's attention?

▶ Is there enough client information?

▶ Do you provide support materials, charts, brochures or leaflets?

Think about developing your team in other ways; do you encourage them to enter competitions? Manufacturers usually sponsor these events, and many will start their selection from an initial photo entry. Competitions are great for team building in the salon and will generate a lot of client interest too. Particularly if the team are highly motivated and talk about the photo shoot with them and the themes that they have in mind.

Remember, all sorts of competitions are popular with the local media, because it is more interesting than reading the 'Court File' or the local supermarket's two for one deal. Everyone is interested in a stage performance, and any form of live entertainment helps to sell newspapers. It makes for good local stories with a positive slant rather than negative, whilst providing the salon with 'free' publicity too.

The expectations of the salon & manufacturer

The **win - win** basis!

Well, things have moved on; products have been trialed and tested; salon staff are starting to use the new references more regularly, the outlook looks good.

So is it smooth sailing at last, or has the circus just left town?

"Well, whilst busy mixing metaphors, we hope it is the former and not the latter."

When everything has been set up, and things are starting to work, we would not want to see the promise of ongoing support, *drift off into the sunset!* The salon would hope that the manufacturer and sales representatives keep up their high standards of service, their *word*, their focus and throughout the whole process.

Naturally, the salon will expect to see an ongoing, standard of service. The *Service Level Agreement (SLA)* should encompass all benefits that the salon receives in respect to purchasing discounts, supporting resources, media coverage, and educational assistance.

Remember, it works both ways - if you have increased your spend or have taken on new product ranges, it is in your supplier's interest to provide ongoing help wherever they can. They know that they are more at risk of other predatory competitors, trying to take your business away than they are of you changing your mind.

The manufacturer will expect some *hick-ups* and maybe a few issues around products, especially with the introduction of new color ranges. They will be ready and prepared to send in help.

In saying this, a salon has to be realistic about its demands when, or if issues arise. We all know that if a group of people uses the same things in the same ways, that they should all get the same results. However, this seldom happens; something within the process is different, and that factor changes the overall outcome. Sometimes for the better, sometimes for worse, but it is not the case for instant alarm or shouting *foul play*. Some things need investigation before *pointing fingers*.

The salon also has to be ready to admit their mistakes, say by improper use or inaccurate application. Blaming the product will not help, give a full and accurate account of what occurred, it would be much easier to track or trace processes that way.

Sadly, the majority of errors occur through:

▸ Mishandling

▸ Inaccurate measurement

▸ Inaccurate mixing

▸ Poor application

▸ Unsuitable hair type/condition

▸ Poor or gapped knowledge

▸ Incompetence

None of which anyone would wish to admit.

Reasonable salon expectations	Reasonable supplier expectations
Timely responses to technical queries	Prompt payment of account
Support for product knowledge and application	Access to regular updates and revisits
Clear instructions for product use	Staff engagement regarding product knowledge, promotion and acceptance
Health and safety information	Safe usage of product in accordance with manufacturer instructions
Ongoing training and support	Salon participation and commitment
Advance knowledge of changes to product ranges, packaging etc.	Increase in sales over time
Samples, customer information, display materials	
Future schedule for planned training, events promotional campaigns, incentives etc.	

3.18

CHAPTER FOUR

WHAT IS A BRAND & DO YOU NEED ONE?

What is a brand?

Many smaller businesses fail to see the significance of this particular topic; they see how it relates to *bigger businesses* but think that it is unlikely to affect them. From a costing point of view, they may be right, as creating a brand from scratch is normally a very expensive exercise.

Typically, a public relations agency *(P.R.)* would only need one contract with a large corporate to bring in plenty of work that will keep them busy and profitably engaged for several years. Therefore, from that standpoint, the amount of hairdressing companies that fall into that international league, can be counted in single figures.

Branding at the top-level; for multi-nationals, is a process for creating a unique identity that enables them to be recognized across the globe. The clever, catchy *strap lines* and artworks; i.e. those that stick in peoples' minds, are usually made up from just a few simple, but expertly designed elements. Current trends in creative design reduce corporate names to a few beautifully crafted abbreviations, a simple logo, or eye-catching color combinations.

Now, I will prove to you that I can read your mind.

Whilst thinking about successful branding; think of a fruit and now take a bite...

Creating a Brand is much more than just thinking about the label on a product it is about developing an identity and ensuring that the identity is *out there* and visible in the landscape.

In the past, successful branding either turned products into household names or made their logos instantly recognizable.

☐ How many people go shopping for a vacuum cleaner, surely, they use another general term instead?

☐ Why do people need a casually drawn *tick* on their leisure footwear?

☐ Which three letters transport parcels around the globe?

☐ If you wanted a cola drink, what well-known drinks spring to mind?

☐ What type of hamburger with relish, cheese, and pickle is available on every continent?

I think that you might be starting to get an idea of where we are going with this. Brand image and the creation of a unique identity has never been more important, and it also applies to you, particularly if you want to stand out from the competition.

So why bother with a salon image at all?

The creation of a brand image is like putting your own 'stamp' on things. It is a trademark that shows who you are (and if it is well designed,) provides a feeling for what you stand for. It signifies the values that you uphold and the quality that you provide within your personal services.

If advertising is about sending a message to potential customers in the hope to do more business with them; then public relations (PR) is about the ways in which that message is communicated. Good PR enhances, channels and directs the advertising message at people who will be interested in hearing about it the most.

This statement may sound a little 'touchy-feely' to you and in 'marketing speak' it is. One of the main reasons that companies spend so much time and money upon their public image is because they want to people to gain a specific view, a feeling about their work and what they do. .

Many large companies find it very difficult to make a direct connection with their customer base because of the nature of their business. For example, the customers of national utilities or banks can only get through to a call center operator to speak to someone about the service that they receive.

Unlike hairdressing or any other personal service industry, the larger corporations (unless they are in retail,) tend to keep customers at *arm's length*. However, in doing this, they realize that it *distances* their operation, making it seem as if they are intangible and unapproachable.

I hope that you can now see why large corporations spend so much time on their brand awareness and public image. Your business relies upon personal service and direct communication, and this gives you a distinct advantage.

The connection that you have with your clients is personal, direct and open - They are only interested in the quality and care that you take in the service that you provide.

However, from an advertising point of view, the hardest thing to express in a *visual way* is feeling, care and sensitivity; this is where branding *steps in* and marketing is everything.

Good Branding is experiential; it enables clients and customers to:

▶ Continue the professional service experience at home

▶ Make then feel better

▶ Cherish the things that they buy and use

▶ Talk with confidence about the people who provided them, with that experience

If you want to create a name for your business and get noticed in your locality, you need people to be talking about you, your business, and what you do.

☑ It creates the public image that you portray

☑ These will become the features that people will recognize and associate with your business

☑ Your brand sets you apart from your competitors

If this introduction has put some new thoughts into your head, or 'chimes' with the beliefs that you already had, then you need to read on...

How does it all work?

It is important to think about what brand creation can do for you, and how it helps the business and your team too. It is essential when planning something of this scale that you take the time to consider and research where your true strengths lie and the underlying values that you uphold.

(See Chapter 2. How well do you know your customers? pgs 17-40 - SWOT Analysis)

Ask yourself what it is that you want to create and what do you expect to achieve.

Remember, **accentuate the positives** *– these are linked to the key strengths of the business, So don't rush this part, you are creating the public face of your business. Both for now and the future, you have to get it right! (Get professional help if you need it – A P.R. consultancy will not necessarily charge for an initial, fact finding consultation).*

Establishing a business that is busy and outwardly successful might be enough for some, but for many others there will be wider horizons and a 'burning' quest for greater success and recognition.

Energy at that level creates the *drive* for privately owned businesses and fuels an entrepreneurial spirit.

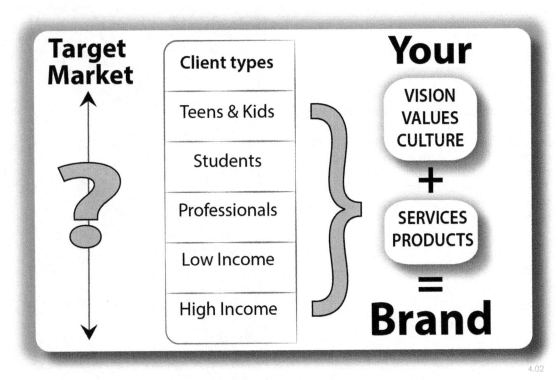

4.02

A vision *(or just a dream?)*

We can all think of things that we want and how we would like things to be, but surely that is day-dreaming...?

What is the difference between daydreaming and having a real vision for your business?

There isn't any difference!

Well, that's not quite true - there isn't a difference between the things that create that mental picture of the future. It is more about the will; determination and perseverance needed in order to make

it happen. If you are realistic about the resources that you have and a good plan for acquiring the others that you need, then you have the basis for a formula for success.

It is those images of the business location, the *décor* the equipment and clients, the variety of services you provide, and the staff that collectively create that vision. That visualization provides a *blueprint* for your brand, one that reflects both you and your aspirations.

Professional PR consultants would take those visible elements and *forge* them together with things that your customers cannot see or do not yet know about you. They will *sift* through your experiences and involvements to find your unique selling points *(USP)* i.e. the assets you possess; that make you and your business unique.

Values

Your innermost values are reflected in the things that you believe in and uphold and the ways in which the staff work together. It provides the 'acid test' for the choices and decisions that you make, and the policy in which staff relate to customers. Quite simply, it is your definition of acceptable standards and what you believe in relation to good business practice.

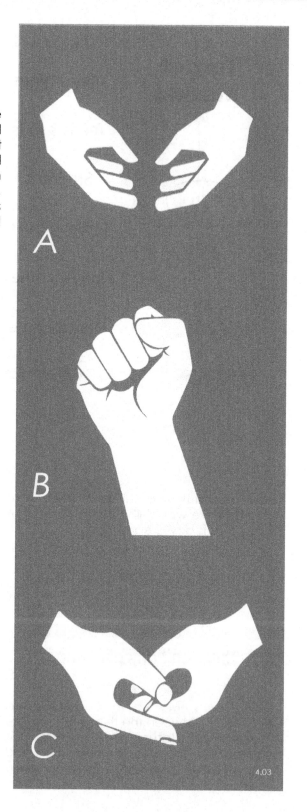

Your values will relate to some or all of the following:

☐ *Fairness and equity*

☐ *Ethics*

☐ *Morals*

☐ *Empathy and concern*

☐ *Knowledge and understanding*

....

"They say - Pictures can paint a thousand words."

....

If you wanted to create a logo that showed people that you would take care of their hair, which of the following images, A, B, or C would you choose?

4.03

Culture

Linked to values; culture, reflects a philosophy for your working environment. It sets the *ambiance;* a background, in which all things take place and the ways in which they function.

This ethos could relate to:

▶ Communication style

▶ Customer services

▶ Openness and honesty

▶ Respect and loyalty

With the suggestion that *Vision, Values,* and *Culture* are the key elements of your brand, then the way that you publicize or broadcast this information to the public becomes the *Branding*. It is your way, the *style* in which you operate and how you market your services or products to customers and clients.

....

Remember, don't be confused with the brands that you sell on behalf of the manufacturer. These products carry their brand, not yours.

....

Plateauing off!

As any business grows, it develops and creates its unique identity. The ethos that has been created by management is cascaded down throughout the team and the external image it projects, becomes the magnet that draws in the clients.

It is *magical* when it works as it creates something that our clients want to be a 'part of.' For them, it would be like joining a members' club where the people associated with it, enjoy it, and the lifestyle and the experiences it provides.

However, most independent salons will reach this point of maturity in their business purely by accident, and that is because all of these things are the outcome or result of the following:

▶ Initial impetus and keenness

▶ Passion and belief in what you do

▶ Energy and enthusiasm

These features are forces; they are the *drivers* that initially kick-start the business. However, taking it to the next level (and stopping the *'plateau effect'* from stemming any further progress) requires a lot more thought and planning.

Getting to know your clients

The key to creating a successful Brand is knowing **who** your customers are in the first place, without this you could be creating:

"A Rolls-Royce for people who can only afford a bicycle."

(If you do not know who your target market is - See Chapter 2 How well do you know your customers? pgs 17-40)

These are the key questions that you need to be able to answer:

☐ Who are the clients that you want to attract?

☐ What are their needs and requirements?

☐ Where are they/will you be able to reach them?

☐ Does your business reflect the type of client you are trying to attract?

Then with the answers, you can start to consider the communication channels that they will respond to

Brand awareness	Communication	
	Methods	**Elements**
Designs / artworks	**In-salon**	➤ Window display ➤ Price lists ➤ Leaflets & brochures
(logos, themes, colors)	**External**	➤ Website ➤ Business stationery ➤ Signs, posters etc.
	Advertising	➤ Newspapers ➤ Magazines ➤ Radio/TV ➤ Internet
Editorial (Written content)	**Social networking**	➤ Facebook ➤ Twitter ➤ YouTube ➤ Blogs etc.

4.04

The initial design elements required for this needs a great deal of consideration, if you want to get your branding right, it needs to be built into everything. *(See table 4.04)*

Work closely with a designer who understands you and your vision and be prepared for some feedback on your ideas. Remember, they know what works from a color and illustration point of view, so listen to what they have to say, as you might be pleasantly surprised. Similarly, if you think that they are *missing* your concept, try putting things another way, take the time to give a full explanation. You do not have to tell them your business plan, but they do need to get a clear idea of where you are aiming.

In a few days or so, your designer will have created two or three design roughs. These will be themes based around your ideas in a variety of styles and done in different color ways; these provide you with choices or *food* for further thoughts.

If you like what you see in their initial roughs, do not make a quick decision, just ask to borrow them for a day or so and get some input from staff and possibly clients as well. You do not have to take their feedback or comments, but they might highlight something that you had not considered.

Finally, when you are happy with one of the themes, you can invite your designer back and talk about how they will be used in each of the elements that you will use for customer communications.

When you finally agree upon the new image, it then becomes the public face of your business. It becomes the *foundation stone* of all advertising, promotion, stationery, website and all social media. If you later expand into multiple outlets or decide to franchise your offering as a mobile service, the logo goes with you.

Remember, the name that you choose, the logo that you have designed, has to be one that represents the team and what you believe, so don't rush into it.

Branding - the bigger picture

If you want people to recognize your brand, then your clients need to be talking about it. Your goal is to reach out and *touch* the clients and share your ethos with them. It will create a symbiosis that connects you with your customers in other ways; beyond what you do for them in their routine hairdressing needs. More importantly, brand awareness is your marketing *vehicle*, it is an identity that created once, is used time and time again in order to reinforce your presence in the wider community. Successful brands are ubiquitous; they are a piece in the *jigsaw* that gives them a position in the business landscape. You only need to look out of the window to be reassured that they are there.

"Some brands are clever by design; others are really clever by design."

No, not a mistake it was intentional.

We know that a good design involves artistic creativity, but there is another marketing strategy that uses wider influences as a method to send messages to potential customers, and this leverages the power of *macro-trends*.

Macro trends are economic indicators caused by changes within a variety of demographics. For example, one particular demographic focusing upon birthrates may illustrate a significant increase in new babies being born in a particular country.

You may feel that this type of information has no bearing on what you do in your business or have any impact on rises or falls in future sales. Unfortunately, you would be wrong; in this instance, a trend showing an increase in birthrates in your country, now has a significant impact on the numbers of people who will be looking at:

☑ Babies / Children's clothing

☑ Baby food

☑ Healthcare

☑ Child benefits and support

☑ Child care, Nurseries, Schools

☑ Parents' work patterns

☑ Holidays, etc.

This illustration does not have an immediate impact upon hairdressing barbering or spa businesses, but shows how the *boom* in one particular demographic, has much wider effect upon everyone.

A forward thinking salon may then think that it would like to capitalize on this trend. They might consider investing in new equipment; such as, a children's' *Soft-Play* area, a *'Story Zone'*, or styling chairs with *'Merry-Go-Round'* animals or cartoon characters.

You still might be thinking that macro trends will have little, or no impact upon you or your business, OK think back to the start of *greener* issues, animal testing, and the everything *organic* revolution. Now you can see the links between what you do in your business and the wider issues of how people are thinking and what they will be experiencing.

There is no point in business, in standing against what the majority of people believe, they will ignore you, and like the *tide*, it will crash over you and wash you away. An individual cannot change a macro trend; it occurs because groups, communities, and populations are all affected or influenced by it.

Quite simply, they are:

☐ Affected by economic and social pressures

☐ Influenced by others in what they are doing and involved with

☐ Sharing in common values, beliefs, and experiences

These key factors influence everything from a choice of religion to mobile phones, and because social networking has enabled people to communicate quickly, the information travels even faster and further. If you want to *surf* on the crest of the waves, you need to be on the *right* trends, at the *right* time.

The table below shows the present macro trends affecting people on a global scale. You can do your own research into finding micro trends affecting your business and potential customers. You can start with your local authority website to find out the numbers of people in your area and the factors that could be influencing their lives and decisions.

Euromonitor International has identified the following ten macro trends as being key vectors to the future growth of consumer markets.

Top-Ten Macro-Trends

1. An uncertain future	*Both political and economic uncertainty are at their highest level for years, and the situation is expected to continue with flow on effects for consumers who in view of uncertain times may well exercise caution when making purchasing decisions.*
2. The emerging middle classes	*The expansion of the middle classes in developing markets has been one of the key outcomes of economic growth, as huge swathes of these populations move out of poverty and form an increasingly demanding and sophisticated consumer base.*
3. The disaffected youth	*One of the key outcomes of the recession for advanced economies is the lack of decent prospects for young people, who face high unemployment, tuition fees, rising living costs, a lack of affordable housing and the burden of supporting ageing populations in the future.*
4. The rich/poor divide	*Inequality has been in evidence for a number of years, but is increasingly becoming a focus of social unrest and media interest. Reasons for inequality include changes in employment patterns, disproportionate wage increases, technological progress, urbanization, government policies and demographic factors.*
5. The climate challenge	*Increasingly erratic weather patterns and rising sea levels will be one of the largest threats to populations over the next five years and beyond. Most notably, droughts and floods will continue to cause havoc with food crops, affecting food prices in the years to come.*

4.05a Source Euromonitor.com (2012-2017)

Top-Ten Macro-Trends

Source Euromonitor.com (2012-2017)

6. An ageing world	*A combination of low birth rates and longer life expectancies is driving the ageing process. Ageing populations will impact future economic growth prospects, due to reduced labour forces and lower savings and investment rates. At the same time, age-related public expenditure is projected to increase strongly.*
7. The urban transition	*Although urbanization is another long-term trend, its pace has speeded up noticeably in recent years and city growth has reached unprecedented levels in emerging markets. The exodus from countryside to cities is largely driven by a desire for economic empowerment. The global shift towards urban living is shaping consumer markets and demand.*
8. People on the move	*As the world becomes smaller, while travel gets cheaper and restrictions more relaxed, more people are choosing to live, study or work abroad. Continued migration has a significant impact on economies, marketers and consumers alike. Greater ethnic diversity offers marketers a wealth of opportunities.*
9. A more connected world	*The Internet is increasingly being accessed via smartphones and tablets, as consumers seek convenience and mobility. Almost one third of global on-line consumers now have internet access on their mobile phones. Social media sites, such as Facebook and Twitter, are changing the way people interact with one another. A successful social media strategy will be a top priority for companies globally.*
10. China goes global	*China's overseas investments were previously concentrated on developing countries and a handful of resource-rich developed economies, such as Australia and Canada, but since 2008 the focus of Chinese investors has begun to shift to North America and Europe. Several Chinese brands have entered the global arena and are looking to challenge the positions of established international brands. Experts expect Chinese companies' investments overseas to see explosive growth in the next decade.*

4.05b

82

Branding on a different scale

When any company name is mentioned, it will either register with the listener or mean nothing at all; it provides two different starting points - **known or unknown**. Which would you rather be?

Knowing what a business does or provides is far more useful than *blind* ignorance. Even if a potential customer does not patronize a business, **knowing about that business and what they do** is vitally important, as it does provide a chance of obtaining new business in the future.

In hairdressing and barbering, this works well; for example, think about how often you get referrals for new customers from people that are not within your clientèle but have heard about you and will:

☑ **Recommend their friends or colleagues to try you out**

☑ **Know that you specialize in particular services and treatments**

☑ **Know that you use certain products that they identify with and possibly use themselves**

Why are we drawn to some brands & not others?

People purchase particular products and services for all sorts of reasons. Sometimes the reasons *seem*, quite shallow and unimportant, on other occasions they make choices that are deeply involved with their personal values, ethics, and beliefs.

We, as amateur marketers, are not here to make judgments we simply observe consumer patterns and produce choices that (hopefully) potential customers will opt to take.

The main *drivers* for brand awareness and loyalty are:

Advertising

The continual marketing and placement of products and services within a variety of public media channels

Peer & Social Pressure

The social pressure by members of one's peer group to take a certain actions, adopt certain values.

Reputation

A history of reliable standards that occur on a repeated basis for satisfied customers

How do I get recognized?

If you think about the three main drivers for brand loyalty, then you might be able to create that awareness and generate the business that goes with it. Admittedly, advertising can be very expensive, and when you attempt a *blended media* approach; using several communication channels, it could be beyond your resources.

The secret is to focus upon those that work best for you and *pool* your resources into making them produce the best yield. For example, if the business was located in a relatively remote geographical location, what would be the point of advertising in the nearest large town's *Evening News*? You may get a far better return on your investment from advertising in your local *Parish Magazine*.

Scaling things up

Not every business will make it into the 'big league' and that is not what this chapter is about. Quite simply, success is a success, and that will be relative to any business size. If the business functions properly, it will *carve out* its market share, and that is how you can measure your success.

Remember there is always a ceiling or saturation point for any business, and that is the point where all the staff are working to their optimal potential.

On the other hand, the scope for mass-produced, manufactured products is far greater, as it is easier to reach a much bigger community. If a globally international company wants to expand and 'scale-up' their business model, the formula for success is far simpler. They simply *buy* the companies in question and with that, their competition's customer base too. It is then just a case of arranging the borrowing from banks or shareholders to make the acquisition.

If we think about international brands that have already made a huge impact in our industry, then we could use the following as an example.

L'Oreal

As a global brand, L'Oreal now encompasses the following companies within the group.

- ☑ Matrix
- ☑ Redken
- ☑ Pureology
- ☑ Body shop
- ☑ Mizani
- ☑ Garnier

There are many others in non-related sectors too, and L'Oreal is partly owned by a company Nestlé with no visible links to the sector.

....

It seems that everyone has their price.

....

The point being made here is that the consumer relates and identifies with the brand and from that; the loyalty is created.

In our example, L'Oreal have created a huge professional and public following, and the brand is known universally.

They say that 'success breeds success,' but what does that really mean?

Well, if you already have a successful business and want to establish your brand image, you are well on the way. If a business is doing well, its reputation is growing and (See table 4.04) that is one of the main cornerstones of good P.R.

Your presence on a local level is just as effective in your community as the other well-known names on the High Street. Your salon becomes the destination for the hairstyling needs of customers that you share with other names such as:

- ☐ W.H. Smiths
- ☐ Marks and Spencer's
- ☐ Tesco
- ☐ Vodafone or
- ☐ Boots

In order to maximize your potential, you need to monopolize at least two out of three key cornerstones; so from that, which other elements do you choose?

- ▸ The pressure that can be applied by groups and communities

- ▸ The coverage achieved by clever advertising campaigns

85

The first one relies upon your clients telling other people and referring your salon as the place to go. It can be done but needs a concerted effort from all the team, all of the time. *(See Chapter 6 Getting staff to start selling pgs 121-150 for more information)*

Another way to do this is through your published customer information, and this can be successful as it starts to overlap into the advertising communication channel as well.

Remember, the advertising route can be very successful but does rely heavily on the message that you want to send.

There are different types of advertising, and some can be more advantageous when building a professional profile, whilst others can often work against you. *It does depend on what you want to achieve and ultimately what you want to sell*

For example, it is one thing sending a subliminal message to potential customers in the way of editorial content. (This can be a newspaper focus upon some salon achievement, or a charity event with which you participated.) It is great for profile building and reputation, but without any specific sales focus, it does not provide any measurable form of financial success.

On the other hand, you may have been able to secure a new range of products that are exclusive to you and you want to promote them in an introductory offer. *Great, **but do you want to be seen (and known) as a discounter?***

Ideally, when it comes to advertising you need a blend of both types of public exposure. You need your efforts and achievements to be published, and your charitable, benevolence recognized, with equal importance. You need to be able to profit from the income derived from specifically targeted sales promotions.

(For more information see Chapter 2 How well do you know your customer pgs 17-40 & Chapter 5 pgs 93-120)

D.I.Y. Design principles

Hair styling business managers and salon proprietors are creative in their own right. Even those who are not currently involved in day-to-day hairdressing or barbering, they probably were at some point previously, and that initiated the thought of *going it alone* in the first place.

This chapter has provided an insight to the bigger corporate picture regarding, local, national and global recognition. It would be an unrealistic expectation for many salons to even contemplate that level of investment, so the following information is a general guide for those considering or attempting their own business *make-over*.

Current thinking in design practice

Intricate, complex Vs simplicity

Hairdressing involves many technical processes that from an observer's standpoint, may look simple and something that they could attempt themselves.

You already know that the work that you do is quite the opposite; it is intricate, time consuming and complex in nature. However, by making it look simple, it encourages others to try and achieve a similar effect.

Less is more... The message here is simplicity. People respond better to something simple rather than complex and this should be reflected in your designs. If you want to send a clear, understandable message to others, then your logo, name and any other public display content needs to be simple, uncluttered and easy to follow.

Color combinations

From an advertising point of view, you only have a few moments to catch the attention of your potential customers and some design elements are definitely better than others.

When designing signs and posters without images, you create a far better impact with fewer colors. Ideally, you should be using colors that have a high contrast so that you make allowances for people who may be visually impaired. Typically, black and darker colors on white will be clearer than lighter shades and pastels.

If you intend to create a range of business stationery for leaflets, price lists, business and appointment cards, then the introduction of one additional 'spot' color works really well for text illustration. For example, black, and (spot color) orange on white, or fresh, 'minty' green work really well.

4.07

Color psychology

There will not be a color or color combination that has not already been used and implying that there are rules for using colors, would be ridiculous. As creative people you use color every day and have a clear idea of what works together and combinations that do not. However, we live in a *world* of color and we can learn so much more from observing patterns that occur in nature.

Yellow

Yellow can provide a feeling of warmth and is always associated with sunshine. This makes it a popular 'feel-good' color and conveys a message of comfort and nostalgia.

However; in nature (and in man-made signs) yellow and black provides a warning of danger and can sometimes be quite stark when used in advertising.

Green

Green has been a popular choice for many years. It is associated with nature and has an *organic,* wholesome feeling that infers freshness and renewal.

In pastel tones it is also used in interior design to convey hygiene and cleanliness and is a popular favourite in Spas, Clinics and Beauty as it provides relaxing environments.

Blue

Similar to green, blues are associated with relaxation, they are the universal tone that depict water and purity.

Again in pastel forms they provide sensual, relaxation when used in interiors.

Red

Strong, bold and fearless, red will always stop people and catch their attention. It is a popular favorite in posters and window display and always provides a clear message for any reader. (Red and black provide the most popular color combination for sale, discounts, promotions etc.

4.08

The value of customer information

As a final note for this chapter, we must never forget the *true* value of accurate customer information.

Q1. Do retailers collect information about their customers? *Yes.*

Q2. Why do retailers collect information about their customers? *Because they want to sell them other things?*

Shopping is a *love-hate* thing, sometimes we want to do it, other times we have to do it, either way, it gives the retailer an opportunity to learn more about us. For example, our purchasing habits; things that we frequently buy and those that we only buy now and again.

From their point of view, the things that we regularly buy, need no promotion or incentive, they could even increase the price a little, and we will still be happy to pay for it. But what about the things that we don't buy very often?

Could they increase their profits if they could get customers to buy a little more often?   Yes.

So, how do they collect and collate customer purchasing habits?

Historically, there was only one way of doing this.

1.   Provide the customers with a loyalty card.

2.   Give them an incentive (e.g. a discount, two for one, or free offers) to use it regularly within the store.

3.   Record the customers' sales data and allocate the information to their loyalty card accounts.

4.   Analyze the information and provide incentives for customers to shop for more of what they buy often and provide more incentives for their less popular items.

Sales opportunities are always customer focused. In other words if you were to apply the adage;

"Which came first, the chicken or the egg?"

In the following scenario:

"Which came first, the product or the customer?"

The answer will always be a ***customer.***

You already know this because; without any customers, there would be no need for any products.

The hair stylist would normally:

☑ Watch the client when they are browsing in the retail area

☑ Notice the things that interest the client

☑ Discuss and recommend suitable products during consultation

How many salons use the information that they have to improve customer services and find alternative ways to sell more?

So, if large retail companies can capitalize on their customers purchasing habits, why can't you?

The illustration below shows how the supermarkets do this.

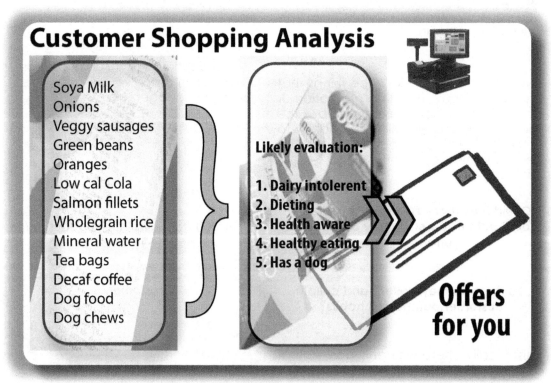

Customer Shopping Analysis

Soya Milk
Onions
Veggy sausages
Green beans
Oranges
Low cal Cola
Salmon fillets
Wholegrain rice
Mineral water
Tea bags
Decaf coffee
Dog food
Dog chews

Likely evaluation:

1. **Dairy intolerent**
2. **Dieting**
3. **Health aware**
4. **Healthy eating**
5. **Has a dog**

Offers for you

4.09

Marketing thoughts:

salon.*Scissors*

salon.S

salon.*Shears*

Setting

salon

salon **Strengths**

5

STARTING TO RETAIL

Starting to retail

The solutions for making a profit

In chapter four, you were introduced to the concept of branding and brand awareness. Within that chapter, you discovered that your brand reflects a variety of features of your business, and this is reinforced by the values that you believe in and uphold. *That vision is now within reach, but you need to make it pay, and successful retailing is one way of realizing the dream.*

If you have not retailed in the salon before, there may be some initial resistance from the staff. *(See Chapter 6. pgs 93-120)* However, this is your business decision, so you will need them 'onboard' very quickly, as you might be getting a few raised eyebrows from the clients and everyone needs to be fully briefed.

Retailing: Things to think about	What are the implications?
The general guideline for a manufacturer's 'mark-up' (excluding any deals) is usually 40%-50%	➤ You cannot ignore the manufacturer's recommended retail price (MRRP) ➤ If you try to **cut** your margins too low, you will need to sell a lot more to make a profit. ➤ If you go **above** the MRRP you might price yourself out of the competition altogether! ➤ If you sell at the MRRP you will need to sell around 2/3rd of the stock **before** you cover your investment.
Attractive displays do not sell products, they need personal recommendation and advice too	Every hair professional is impressed by a well-designed, attractive retail display. Try to see beyond the cool lighting and fashionable fittings. You might think that it is a fabulous addition to your salon, but your clients will see this as the standard of shop fitting they see everywhere. *Why should yours stand-out to them?*

If you buy products because you like the color themes, packaging and overall image, you would be better off saving your money and redecorating instead

> Product design is customer focused and particularly suited to specific types of customer. For example, the simplicity of product uniformity, say, in white or pastel packaging will appeal differently to that of client that likes bold, contemporary fashion effects.

> Do not choose products because they coordinate with the color of your towels or the tiles on the floor. They must be selected because they meet the needs of your clientèle.

Remember, your staff sell the products and they will need an incentive

The price **mark-up** should accommodate the 'costs-of-sales' too. In other words, it should provide sufficient returns to provide a profit **and** cover a commission.

5.01

Salon floor plans & layouts

There are so many things to consider when thinking about or planning a retail area in your salon, and it all depends on your budget. **Yes, the purchases made with the intention of selling at a profit are an asset, but only if you sell them!**

However, do not let this put you off, the business model that incorporates a retail shop for hair and beauty products can be *really* big business. If you can build a good repeat business for retail and become the preferred choice for your clients' hair maintenance needs, then you could see your profitability on the annual accounts double in just one year!

The first thing that you have to consider before anything else is your available space. Even if you have planned and budgeted for a sales area, it must fit your existing work areas.

Yes, retail is an asset to the business, and it can produce some excellent returns on investment, but unless it enhances your existing service provision, you may be 'Robbing Peter to pay Paul'. In other words, you need to add retail as a feature to the business, but not at the cost of losing any other valuable workspace.

Workflow - *the way in which processes are connected*

The first considerations are your workflows and traffic routes; the following illustrations look at these two important aspects.

Workflow – *the sequence of salon processes that create your salon services*

Traffic routes – *the physical routes taken by staff and clients in providing those salon services*

The model below provides a typical workflow for several salon processes. There may be several people involved within this sequence, but the process is the same:

1. The client is received and made welcome; their appointment is checked, and they are offered something to drink and read whilst they wait

2. The hair stylist conducts a personal consultation; they find out what the client wants and assesses whether this is achievable by carrying out an examination of the client's hair and skin. They then confirm the desired outcome or make recommendations based upon their assessment and agree a suitable course of action

3. The client's hair is prepared for the agreed services, and the technical processes are carried out to achieve the desired outcome

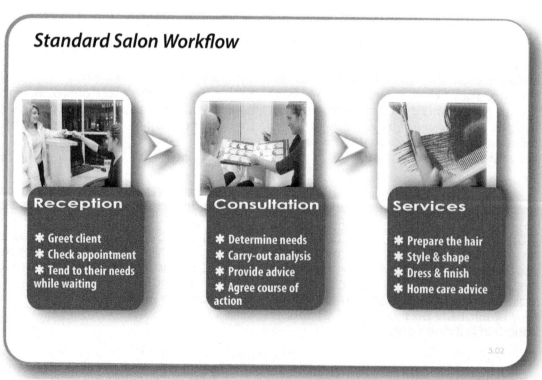

Standard Salon Workflow

Reception
* Greet client
* Check appointment
* Tend to their needs while waiting

Consultation
* Determine needs
* Carry-out analysis
* Provide advice
* Agree course of action

Services
* Prepare the hair
* Style & shape
* Dress & finish
* Home care advice

5.02

The 3 stage sales strategy:

Stage 1.
At reception

The passive sales approach

The client arrives at reception and the receptionist greets the client and checks their appointment and asks them to take a seat

➤ The client stands within the retail area and can see the variety of products that are on sale

➤ Whilst the client is waiting they notice the current promotions and can find out more by reading the brochures and leaflets that are within easy reach

➤ The client is tempted to sample the current promotion

Stage 2.
During consultation

The prescriptive sales approach

The stylist conducts a consultation with the client to:

☑ Determine their requirements

☑ To see if there are any limiting factors

☑ Agree a course of action

➤ The client explains what they want

➤ The stylist assesses whether the desired outcome is achievable

➤ The stylist recommends suitable products that will make hair maintenance easier

Stage 3.
During the technical services

The demonstration & personal experience approach

The salon team carry out a variety of technical services to achieve the desired effects

The client is able to handle and experience the products that are placed within easy reach

➤ The shampooist uses the prescribed products at the basin

➤ The hair stylist uses the prescribed products during the styling services

➤ The client can hold the product, smell the fragrance, look at the ingredients and ask questions about it

5.03

This basic service workflow covers all of the salon processes and provides a standard of service for which, the clients are happy to pay. It also provides opportunities for making additional sales at each of the steps within the sequence – i.e. *the salon's standard service*

The message within this particular illustration shows that you can 'tailor' your sales tactics within your salon's workflows to suit your particular salon. If we take a moment to look back at the table (fig 5.03), we see that sales opportunities arise in all three steps:

Ideally, all three steps would be used as a strategy for generating sales. That way, the client will never feel *pushed* into a quick sale. The service experience will be optimized, and products have a prominence throughout the whole salon service. *The 3 stage sales strategy* is perfect for any personal service industry as it takes the client through a variety of smooth, seamless transitions to a mutually beneficial conclusion.

You need to remember that no other shopping experience offers this type of sales technique or provides a similar sales experience.

This type of *'warm'* selling opportunity is based upon:

▶ Personal recommendation

▶ Professional expert advice

▶ *'Try before you buy'* personal experiences

Traffic routes – *the ways in which services are connected*

Very few hairdressers (or barbers for that matter) consider the client's journey. Admittedly, the traffic flows within barber's shops are far simpler than hairdressing salons, and that is because virtually all the barbering services are provided from the same seating location.

Hairdressing differs greatly from barbering, and it's not because we want to keep our clients running around our salon floor plan, it is because of the nature of the services being offered.

From the client's point of view, an interesting salon layout is *'eye candy'* because the layout and physical boundaries of the salon are intriguing, and different décor themes can obscure the different service areas. Mirrors, workstations, and room divisions provide many different opportunities for lighting effects, moods, and settings.

Yes, we want the client to feel comfortable in their surroundings, but not to the extent where they feel like they could be at home on the sofa!

We want the salon surroundings to be interesting, but again, not to an extent where someone would feel conspicuous. For example, imagine how they would feel if they had to *'strut along a catwalk'* to the basin or *'mount the stage'* to sit at a workstation. What if they felt uncomfortable sat looking at themselves, in a large, *grandiose* mirror?

We know that people can get used to anything, given time, but we must never forget that:

▸ First impressions count

▸ Relaxing environments put clients at ease

These two factors are essential for creating the right salon ambiance; moreover, they are fundamental for creating the right selling environment too.

Quite simply, sales have a lot to do with psychology and if you remember your *'feng shui'* then the whole design aspect of buildings are implicit in the ways in which people respond and experience them. How do you want your salon to be experienced by your customers; as a *military obstacle course* or a *fairy grotto?*

The choice is yours and goes a lot further than your retail areas.

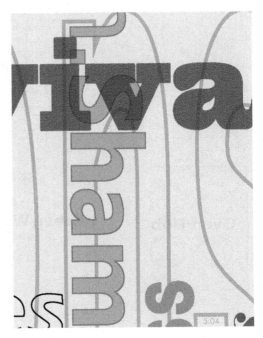

How do other sectors tackle the workflow/traffic route design factors?

Workflows are important in every sphere and if we take kitchen design as an example; a professional design consultant focuses upon three specific work areas that form the main hub of the kitchen. These three items are fundamental to the smooth operation of kitchen routines and affect everything that happens within the kitchen. Therefore, the three locations are connected to form a triangle, and because they affect everything that can take place within the kitchen, the shortest possible traffic route must connect them together.

The following illustration shows the kitchen work triangle and focuses upon the sink, oven/hob, and refrigerator as being the most important areas within the room.

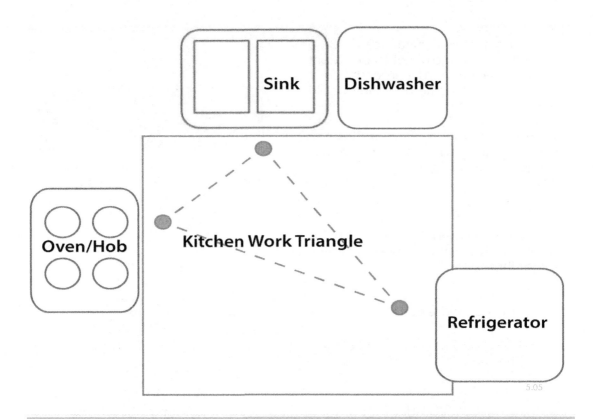

Sink

Dishwasher

Oven/Hob

Kitchen Work Triangle

Refrigerator

5.05

Differences & similarities within workflows & traffic routes

The kitchen is used primarily for domestic use whereas a salon is used for public services

People need to be able to move around both with ease and the main areas of focus should be connected instinctively, i.e. logically through common sense

The kitchen is a room with a primary function for preparing food although it becomes a focal point for everyone for many other reasons

A hair salon is a business with a primary function for creating an income although it provides a social centre, a place of relaxation and provides an uplifting experience for the customers

The kitchen (from a design point of view) is one of two main reasons (the other being the bathroom) that attracts people when moving house or flat

The look and image of a salon is one of two main reasons (the other being recommendation) that attracts new customers and encourages them to visit

5.06

These three points form frequent destinations for anyone preparing food and should be clear of any obstacles that might create a hazard, or affect a smooth operation.

You may be thinking; "what has this got to do with a salon?" Well, the same principles apply, but this time with a different focus. Look back at the table to see how similar the processes are.

Salon floor plans & traffic routes

Designing, the traffic flows in a salon, is vitally important and as varied as the number of buildings available. For example, designing a traffic flow for premises within a period building is very different to that within a modern shopping complex. The older style building would not have been built with the purpose that you have in mind, let alone the shop fitting that needs to take place in order to make it work.

In many ways, the modern 'box-like' retail lock-up within a shopping complex is far easier to plan. It may not have the quirkiness or appeal of the period property, but it will be simpler to setup. However, by the very nature of *building over time*; there are far more legacy period properties in towns than there are shopping malls. Therefore, when the salon location means everything, you sometimes have to settle for the tougher option.

In the section relating to workflows, we discovered that a basic salon model has three processes creating our salon service, we also find out that there are three locations within our kitchen work triangle.

The three-step process is not a coincidence; it is the ideal working template by neither being too long nor too short. In the following illustrations, we change the destinations for those in an effective/efficient working salon.

In our first illustration *(fig 5.07)*, we see a typical rectangular floor plan, and the reception desk faces the front door. The client is received at reception and waits in the nearby seated area where the consultation takes place. The client can see the shampoo area from the waiting area and moves to the basins and then to the workstation to receive the salon services.

The same traffic route occurs in the next illustration, but this time over a larger salon layout.

Sometimes the ideal traffic route is compromised because of the physical layout, and in these situations, common sense has to prevail. In the next illustration, we see a narrow salon floor plan, in this scenario, it is not possible to site the shampoo area near to the reception, so a different route has to be taken.

The reception area is always located at the front of the salon. Therefore, it is on full view from the entrance or the front window; this is naturally the focal point of the shop and from outside everything is on show to any passersby.

Traffic routes

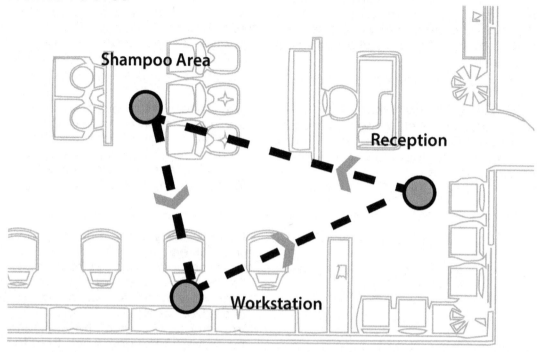

5.07

5.08

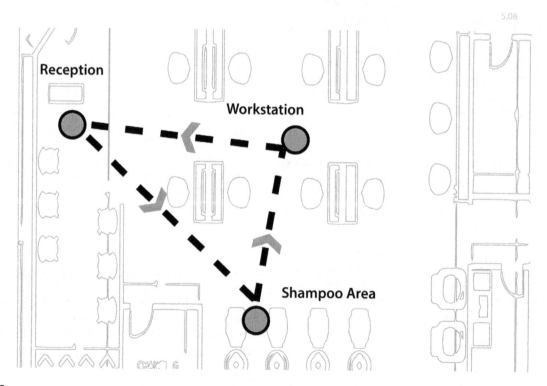

Traffic routes cont.

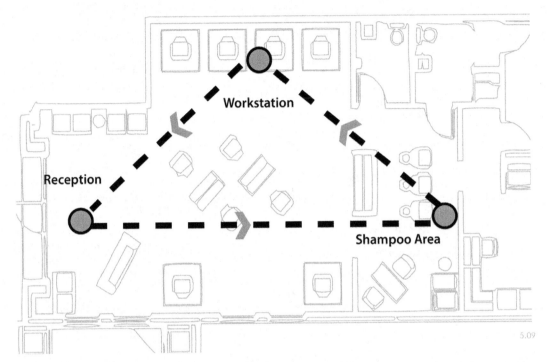

5.09

As a rule, people do not mind being seen at a workstation having their hair done, but lay-back at the basin; having their hair shampooed is another matter.

Therefore, in our third illustration above, (fig 5.09), the traffic route triangle remains the same, but the client will make a longer journey to avoid being seen from the front of the shop.

Sales 'hot spots'

When you have determined the traffic routes through the salon based upon the workflow processes, the next thing, to consider, are the sales *hot-spots*. The sales *hot-spots* are the zones and areas within your salon that support the **passive sales strategy.** (See figs 5.11,13,14) These areas create visual prompts and stimulate an interest within the client that should form the basis for conversation between them and their hair stylist. If you have drawn a plan of your salon, you can do a virtual walk-through to see where sales *hot-spots* should be located.

The *hot-spots* can take the form of *in-salon product displays*, or in situations where space or security does not permit this - then it could be an ideal location for a *poster display* or some other written information.

If we take another look at our three example floor plans, we can now highlight the sales hot-spots and the types of promotion that could take place.

103

Salon example 1.

Hot spot	Location	Promotional materials	Aims & objectives
A	**Magazine table**	Leaflets	Customers have the chance to read and think about your promotional offer in relative privacy
		Brochures	Stimulates interest and could prompt questions later
B	**Retail Display Cabinet**	Products	Customers are attracted to well-lit displays and have the opportunity to handle the products
		Posters	Posters can support existing TV, Radio, Magazine, Newspaper campaigns and this reinforces coverage and branding
		Shelf talkers	Moving signs showing spot promotions that stand out
C	**Reception point**	Products	Individual product or promotional display focusing upon the salon's current promotion
		Posters	Posters can support existing TV, Radio, Magazine, Newspaper campaigns and this reinforces coverage and branding
D	**Shampoo area**	Banners / signs	Helps to reinforce branding like posters, but can give the client something to look at whilst lay back at the basin
E	**Workstation**	Leaflets	Customer can pick up leaflets and take them home
		Products	Customers can handle the products, smell the contents and discuss the features and benefits with their hair stylist

5.10

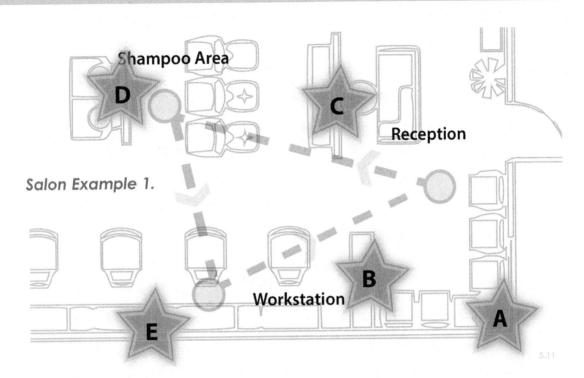

Salon Example 1.

Salon example 2.

Hot spot	Location	Promotional materials	Aims & objectives
A	Magazine table	Leaflets Brochures	Customers have the chance to read and think about your promotional offer in relative privacy. Stimulates interest and could prompt questions later.
B	Window display	Products Posters	Customers are attracted to well-lit displays and this forms a topic for conversation. Posters can support existing TV, Radio, Magazine, Newspaper campaigns and this reinforces coverage and branding
C	Shampoo area	Banners / signs	Helps to reinforce branding like posters, but can give the client something to look at whilst lay back at the basin.
D	Workstation	Leaflets Products	Customer can pick up leaflets and take them home. Customers can handle the products, smell the contents and discuss the features and benefits with their hair stylist.

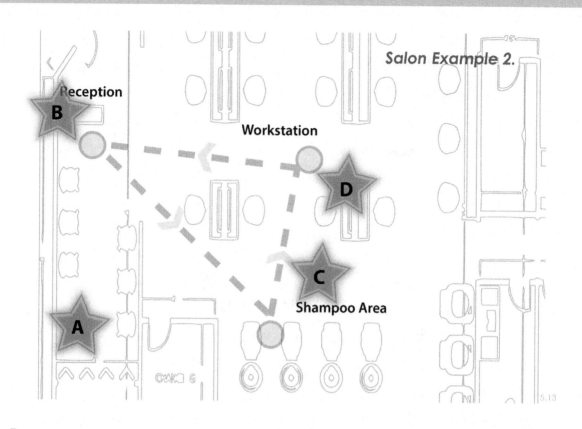

Salon Example 2.

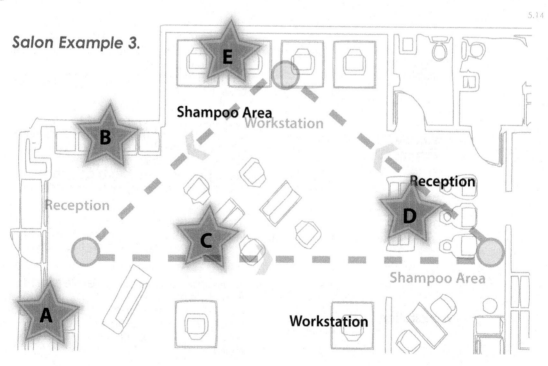

Salon Example 3.

Salon example 3.

Hot spot	Location	Promotional materials	Aims & objectives
A	Window display	Products Posters	Customers are attracted to well-lit displays and this forms a topic for conversation Posters can support existing TV, Radio, Magazine, Newspaper campaigns and this reinforces coverage and branding
B	Waiting area	Leaflets Brochures	Customers have the chance to read and think about your promotional offer in relative privacy Stimulates interest and could prompt questions later
C	Workstation ends or display shelving	Products	Individual product or promotional display focusing upon the salon's current promotion
D	Shampoo area	Banners / signs	Helps to reinforce branding like posters, but can give the client something to look at whilst lay back at the basin
E	Workstation	Leaflets Products	Customer can pick up leaflets and take them home Customers can handle the products, smell the contents and discuss the features and benefits with their hair stylist

5.15

Everyone is stimulated by something new, the feeling may not last long, but the initial impact is strong and exciting. This feeling is part of human psychology, and you can play this to your advantage, but only if you get your timing right.

If you have a regular, repeat custom business, you will be seeing your clients at least once every six weeks or so. They may be returning sooner than this, but at worst, they will be coming back every couple of months. Working further with this principle, you should be keeping your salon promotions fresh in the mind of your clients. Get them used to seeing new things, and they will be eager to talk about them during their visits.

You should plan your year ahead in your diary so that you cover one promotional campaign every two months. That means that you have six to plan for throughout the year and plenty of time during each campaign to arrange your display materials and order your products for the next one.

If you work closely with the manufacturer, it could prove really useful. They would be able to give you advance notice of their national advertising campaigns, and you will be able to plan ahead for these events and prepare for them accordingly. For example, magazine advertising is usually booked a season in advance so your manufacturer will be able to help you with the point-of-sale material, as well as the correct stock.

Work with the available space

The size and layout of your salon you should always be the first consideration when planning to set up your in-salon retail area. If your salon is small, you may only have enough space for a few shelves and a limited amount of stock. If the salon size is large, it will allow for a complete 'one stop shop' retail area which can offer many different brands and products.

After giving some consideration to your available space, you should make some decisions about the amount of retail shelves or display units you can physically fit in. Running shelf space is referred to in length terms and refers to your product display as 'metreage or footage.' (This term simply means the length of shelf space you have.) Manufacturers tend to work this way because their marketing departments create visual planograms of shelving with the ideal set standards for product display.

If your manufacturer provides you with a planogram, use it, as this will take a lot of guesswork out of the equation, and provide you with clear instructions on how to build successful professional merchandising operation.

A typical planogram for a retail product display

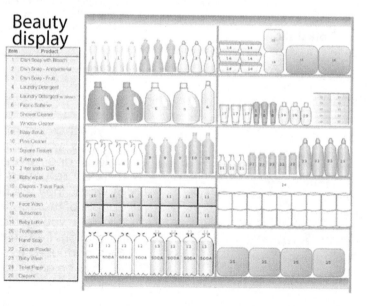

The length of shelving depends on the amount and range of products that you want to sell. You need to think about the following:

- ☑ *Number of product lines*
- ☑ *Amounts of each product*
- ☑ *Accessories, jewellery, and ornamentation*
- ☑ *Styling tools and equipment*
- ☑ *Hair extensions and associated items*

In chapter 3 we discussed salon and the supplier and as part of this topic, we looked at stocking levels.

Remember you do not necessarily need six of everything on display all of the time, this is 'dead money' on the shelf until sold. Many salons will choose to have a well-stocked retail display often with dummy products instead; this supports the merchandising approach to selling, but greatly reduces your stock-in-hand investment. Salons that do this will also use dummy products in their main window and product displays; that way, they can keep their working stock elsewhere and ready for sale.

Things to remember:

Don't	Forget the salon identity or lose your focus, the retail side of the business needs to complement the services that the salon offers.
Do	Some research on the products that your clients are asking for and do your *homework* on the competition; what are they selling and how much are they charging for it?
Don't	Be drawn into a discount price wars, remember you are catering for your *target market* and the retail sales are just a part of the overall service.
Do	Keep you display area interesting whatever the size, be it one shelf or a full designated retail area highlight products, If you have an in-salon product promotion make sure all the staff are *on-board* and talking about it.
Don't	Be greedy with pricing, yes it needs to make money and you have to pay commissions, but don't price yourself out of the market.
Do	Remember that it is better to sell lots of products for a small profit than only one product for a large profit!
Don't	Clutter your retail area with too much stock posters or displays it can look very amateur and *tacky*.

S.17a

109

Don't	Be tempted to over-order stock, remember its only making money when it's moving off the shelf. Monitor and keep a healthy working stock replenish regularly always thinking and planning ahead especially when considering promotional offers and seasonal offers that can greatly increase the retail sales figures.
Do	Not lose sight of your marketplace; consider the consumers' demands and keep a focus upon what's hot and what's not.
Do	*Look after number 1* if you have your own label brand, consider whether you need to carry a manufacturer brand as this offer clients extra choice and could be a direct competition.
Do	Make sure all products clearly priced
Do	Make sure that the staff are fully trained and knowledgeable about the promotions and stock

5.17b

Schemes & themes

The salon décor themes are one of the main considerations for many new proprietors, and the decisions that they make, are often flawed. Most new salon owners choose their decoration and styling based upon the things that they would like to *live in*, rather than work in, and this can have many costly long-term implications!

The materials (that they choose) may be effective and stylish but generally, not suitable for commercial use:

Color choice and themes can have a big impact upon your clients and in ways, you may have not considered before. Retail and selling is a science, it has a formula that when you get it right, it all works for you. So think before you reach for the can of red paint!

When you look at any large retail chain store, you see that they choose one theme and stick to it; as their branded image throughout all of their outlets. They may often choose bright, bold, primary color combinations, but their subliminal intention is to keep you awake whilst you shop. A color scheme like this may work for them, but would be far too busy for a relaxing salon environment.

In contrast to retailers, a perfumery concession or a beauty franchise, has a very different ambiance for its customers. A perfumery will often choose rich colors and lavish finishes within their theming, such as purple and maroon, or precious metals like gold, or silver.

In the beauty salon or spa, they want to convey a clinical, hygienic feeling and one associated with white walls, opaque glass and relaxing pastel blues or greens.

Flooring

Fashionable flooring tends to be for light domestic use such as tiled effects, feature flooring, laminate flooring.
Commercial sheet flooring tends to be serviceable but uninteresting from a design and visual point of view.

Shelving

Attractive, colored shelving will be made from laminates that are suitable or ornaments and books, but not damp, wet towels, or spillages and chemical products.
Shop-fitted quality shelving is hard wearing but limited in fashionable finishes or colors.

Occasional furniture

Stylish furniture is often made from composite wood fiber or pulp and is not strong enough or **safe** enough for public use.

Wall coverings

Wallpaper and textiles can look good but may have a dramatic impact upon the size and shape of the rooms and will affect how a customer experiences their salon visit.
Busy backgrounds may be visually stimulating but will tend to conceal or mask in-salon promotions, products and point of sale.

Lighting

Accent lighting – for illuminating work areas, work stations and product or retail displays

Non-commercial lighting is not suitable for salon layouts.
The variety of low voltage LED or halogen fitments may seem bright but have an optimal distance from the bulb in which to illuminate an object. Mains voltage spot lights do have a higher capacity to illuminate an area well, but are not cost effective and will produce a lot of heat.
Commercial ceiling lighting tends to be fluorescent or LED strip lighting mounted into panels with reflective baffles – good overall lighting but poor for illuminating a mirror or workstation from above for technical work.

Ambient lighting – for illuminating backgrounds and creating moods within room settings

Non-commercial lighting can be used for creating moods within room settings i.e. up-lighters, down-lighters, wall lights etc.
They can create attractive effects for basin areas, relaxation areas and displays.

5.18

111

You might want the glass and chrome look with polished steel in your salon but does it suit your target market? Is it inviting or will it put them off?

Some may like it and have an affinity with your design sense, but others may see it as a suggestion of high style and high prices, is this what you want?

Remember, the first impression is a lasting one and above all, you need it to be the right impression.

Merchandising the retail solution

When it comes to selling volumes of products, you need to be watching the companies that can do it well; they have to succeed with retailing. Otherwise, they go out of business!

Historically, the hair industry has not embraced the sale of products as a valid business strategy. Many see it as a side-show, and not something that they could, or should be involved in; they are often more concerned about:

1. Size of personal investment
2. **Staff commitment / involvement**
3. **Initial training / education**
4. Lack of control

Nevertheless, if these are the only barriers to a huge growth potential for your business - *is considering retail too much to ask?*

Two of these four factors are covered comprehensively within this book; the other two areas are undefinable because they relate directly to you. In *Chapter 2 pgs 17-40* you found out how **SWOT** analysis is used to identify strengths and weaknesses, and then how these can affect your opportunities and threats in business. The process can be quite revealing but misses one thing that all successful hairdressers have in common.

The one great strength, which all hair stylists share is the latent skill of being able to find practical solutions to theoretical problems, and you do this each day in your work. You do this so quickly and instinctively that you forget about it all together. The work involved within hair styling and barbering is easy to evaluate. You use a range of tools and equipment, in a variety of techniques and applications, to achieve an infinite amount of different outcomes and effects.

In other words, you do the right job for each and every client. The difference between the *consummate* professional and the novice is something called experience; - the time-served practice of doing things repeatedly until you:

☑ *Learn how to tackle complex technical procedures*

☑ *Do the right things at the right time, correctly, on every occasion*

In order for a hair stylist to find a practical solution for their clients, they have a *buffer moment* a sort of '*reset button*', which enables them to:

> ▸ Stop and disengage from what they were doing before

> ▸ Clear their mind of the other tasks they are handling

> ▸ Focus upon the needs of the client they have before them

> ▸ Work out what they can do for them

> ▸ Work out how they are going to achieve it

....

This magical process is called consultation. You know this is true because if you miss this part out or do not do it properly, things will invariably go wrong.

....

What is merchandising?

There are distinct advantages to the merchandising approach and hairdressing product manufacturers have now copied the tried and tested methods of successful retailers and will pass on those secrets to you.

Merchandising can be explained in the following way:

In supermarkets, product groups have a set pattern in which they laid out; this helps us, as shoppers, to locate and find what we want to buy. Professional retailers know that in order to make good returns on their retail sales.

They need to:

> ▸ Make shopping easier by helping customers to buy what they want

> ▸ Encourage customers to buy other things as well

For example. Imagine going into a supermarket to buy a sandwich for your lunch. But whilst you look at the range of fillings, you notice that if you spend a little bit more, you can get a drink and a savory snack too. In other words, you went in to buy one thing, but found that the retailer had already considered your needs and thought you might want to buy the item as part of a complete meal.

The strategy occurring in that scenario is called '*up-selling*' and could have worked in several other ways. Whilst you were looking along the shelves for something to eat for your lunch, you notice the latest edition of your favorite magazine. It is not the normal location for the magazine, but you do have the time to browse because you want to take your lunch into the park today. Therefore, you buy the magazine along with the 'meal deal' and set off in the direction of the park to relax. You had not only been *up-sold* from a sandwich to a drink and snack too, you have also been '*cross-sold*' to a non-food item that you had not even considered.

113

Keeping *'tabs'* on your investment:

Preparation	*What are the plans & decisions that have to be made before you start?*	➤ Researching the ranges, options & suitability of products for your target market ➤ Choosing a product range & supplier ➤ Negotiating a package of support, staff education, promotion ➤ Investigating the terms and conditions ➤ Planning the introduction & advertising support
Finances	*How much available money do you have, will you need to borrow in order to make the necessary purchases?*	➤ New products are 'stock in hand' and accounted for as an asset to the business, but do you have the money available or are you speculating that you can 'trade' the costs within your accounting year? ➤ Equipment & furniture has to be bought for displaying and keeping your products secure. This will be tax deductible but subject to depreciation over time
Time	*What sorts of time-scales should you allow?*	➤ Staff development – getting them trained & ready to be able to sell effectively ➤ In getting a return on your investment
Commitment	*How much hard work & effort is needed to make the venture a success?*	➤ Are you expecting a quick return or looking to the longer term? ➤ Are you capable of sustaining the energy for the duration? ➤ Do you generally get fed-up or bored with things very quickly?

5.19

Knowing your customer and understanding their needs is the key to operating a successful business. When merchandising techniques are implemented correctly, there are so many ways to increase the customers' spend.

Supermarket merchandising

When we use a particular supermarket, we get used to the layout i.e. we know that as we enter, we first see the newsagent's kiosk selling papers, magazines, tobacco, and confectionery. Moving on through the store, we find the fresh produce market stalls. Somewhere close at hand are the delicatessen, the bakery, the fishmongers and the butchers.

In-between, we find tinned foods, dairy produce and so on. These are laid out in a specific style. On each of the product shelves, families of products appear. These products are positioned edge to edge and several items deep.

An appearance of uniformity

There is a professional way to display your stock, and hairdressing manufacturers would like salons to adopt this approach. In principle, the concept is quite straightforward. You create a clearly defined area, with an attractive, *well-lit* display, this should provide a comprehensive range of options for your clients, with shampoos, conditioners, treatments, and styling.

Products are placed edge to edge in color-coordinated groupings on purpose built shelving, this will encourage clients to

shop when they visit your salon, and this is good business. Elsewhere within the salon the *message* can be reinforced by creating attractive displays, this will encourage clients to talk about products and ask their stylist for advice.

This approach to salon merchandising provides a professional image, but it can be expensive from a stock holding position.

Merchandising products in this way sells in measured units; each metre of product shelving will be filled edge to edge and several products deep, it eliminates the need for additional storage since the shelves become your storeroom. Merchandising is an ideal option for creating an *in-salon* shop and providing a prescriptive alternative to the supermarket store.

'Savvy' selling in the future

The hair industry may be at the forefront of fashion, but it does tend to be towards the 'back of the cue' when it comes to embracing information technology. Competition is tough and modern merchandising is about to take another step closer to its customers.

New software developed for (optical) retina scanning, will be able to monitor the customer and their preferences whilst they are actively shopping. In the clothing sector, electronic surveillance technology will be able to see what customers are looking at by mapping their eye movements.

Moreover, when a customer spends more time looking at one particular item than another, it will be assumed, (quite correctly) that they are genuinely interested. This display of interest or 'buying signal' is then interpreted electronically to display the item and all its features, color options, pricing, etc. on an overhead promotional screen. A Q.R. code is displayed and scanned by the customer's smartphone and purchasing options quickly appear.

Creating an attractive in-salon shop

Make the most of your available space. If you cater for both men and women; try to differentiate, have an area that caters for each. Men tend to shop differently to women and can be easily distracted or *put-off*. So make it easy for them, place your male orientated products such as styling gels, mud, pastes, and varnishes in one area. Group your products in logical sequences, place shampoos next to conditioners and styling next to finishers. By displaying in this way, you create a 'one-stop-shop' solution for everyone's needs. If you have enough space, you could create a male display area with a table, shaving mirror, razor, and comb; as men often lack the same level of imagination. *They often need to see 'the bigger picture' of what is on offer first, before they buy it all!*

Focus on the important things, if you are 'tight' on space then position the most popular and beneficial products in the prime, visible location.

Product placement

Supermarkets spend a fortune in researching into the ways in which people shop, and they will regularly switch complete product settings around so that we have to navigate past the things that we would not normally see.

Eye level is Buy-Level and for obvious reasons. The premium placement area for any product is on the upper and top shelves as this prompts people to pick up products and find out more. Conversely, the main focal points for younger children's *'pester pound'* is on lower shelves as they can find (and reach) things that interest them.

Shelf-talkers will be located in the décor edge-stripping of the upper shelves as their nodding habit uses movement as a means of distraction. They will often show 'spot' promotions or important information and the message here is *'look at me.'* They work on the principle that there is very little time to capture a customers' attention, so movement brings an additional dimension to a potential sale.

Smells are in important channel of communication too. Have you ever wondered why the coffee shop, or the in-store bakery are both located near the front of the store? The smells of freshly baked bread, or the *barista* brewed coffee creates a compelling urge to buy. The smells and fragrances of hair products are an important feature too. Hair product manufacturers consider this to be a major selling point and expect our clients to pick-up and smell a product's fragrance as this is one of the primary impulse *drivers* for creating a sale.

How many times do you hand a client a product whilst they sit at the workstation and watch them remove the top to take a sniff?

With these principles in mind, you can start to see that the placement of products is more science than art, so stop treating them like wallpaper!

Get out the calendar

Remember to 'mark up' your calendar in advance. If your promotional campaigns work on a six or eight weekly basis, do not miss the opportunities to link your products to specific calendar events or dates. Christmas may be an obvious one, but there are many different festivals running across a variety of different cultures. Each one is special and has personal meanings for those concerned.

Remember, even if your products can not be linked to an event, your displays can show your openness, awareness and empathy of other significant cultural occurrences.

Tuned in - switched on

Many salons use TV as a promotional aid within the salon, and a wall mounted TV in the reception area can provide a lot more than general entertainment. TV is ubiquitous, and (where it may have been frowned upon in the past,) it now plays a useful part in supporting your brand image, as well as product promotions. There are many channels available on subscription as well as Internet and DVDs that focus upon hairdressing and hair fashion themes. If this theme fits in with your salon's particular image, then it can provide an engaging alternative to written information or poster campaigns.

You do need to look into the cost of supporting the media throughout the year and also check if the content supported by the video or the streams work with your particular product lines. The last thing that you need is an all singing and dancing platform that is promoting *your competitor's product ranges!*

Some salons offer free *Wi-Fi* with *tablets* for their clients to use whilst having their hair done. These can be pre-programmed initially to display styles, images and product information associated with your salon's services and ranges.

But remember, in being forward thinking you do need to consider what works best for you and your target market. Gimmicks can be fun, but unless they are contributing to the rent, they have very little value in helping you to develop (or pay for) your business!

Customer information

The handouts and preprinted information like leaflets and brochures, supplied by manufacturers are always well presented and produced in a way that is very *handy* and easy to read. Never turn down the option of taking the manufacturers' printed information as opposed to producing your own.

Their marketing departments spend a lot of time *polishing* their customer information so that the benefits are 'plain to see' and that the all-important small print, with *legalese*, complies with all statutory and regulatory requirements.

Remember, if you are producing your own materials to support your own brands, make sure that you work with someone who can advise on the content, layout and wording.

Events to consider:

New Year's Eve

Chinese New Year

Easter

Mother's day

Father's day

Independence day

Eid – at the end of Ramadan

Yom Kippur

Diwali – festival of light

Halloween

Thanksgiving

Christmas

5.20

What to write, what to avoid

Creating a price list or tariff of salon services is one thing, but producing written information that will be taken away and read at some later time, is quite another.

Our clients are used to the marketing and advertising campaigns run by the manufacturers on the Internet, TV, radio and monthly magazines. If they come into your salon asking about the products that you sell and that they have seen, it can only make your job a lot easier.

Our clients know their basic hair needs and read about them in a variety of on-line blogs, discussion groups, and magazine articles. They know what they want, so you need to stay one step ahead.

Trade & trading

Please see Appendix A on pgs 167-169 at the back of this book for websites and addresses for more information for UK, USA Canada & Australia.

Some things to remember when producing your own customer information:

Do make sure that any written material is technically and grammatically accurate.

Don't get anything printed until it has been proof read by someone else.

Do pay attention to any product claims and remember to cover them as a list of features and benefits.

Don't make any written claims or inferences that are not part of the manufacturer's specification for that particular product.

Do list product ingredients if you really want to, but remember that most scientific info is boring and *nerdy*.

Don't make any false associations with chemical formulations E.g. *'Contains no bleach'* may be accurate, but what chemical compound replaces the bleach in order to make it work?

Do try to write in a light and *chatty* informal way. People are far more likely to warm to that style rather than a dull, factual recital.

Don't use comical or illegible fonts in your printed information. It can convey the wrong impression, even if you think they are great.

Do use headings, sub headings and short paragraphs of information, bullet points are good and so are tables. *(Unlike me, you're not writing a book and you need to capture peoples' attention)*

Don't try to cram too much information on to a page or leaflet just because you can. Font size needs to be open and large enough to be clearly understood by anyone who reads it.

Do try to talk to your audience through your information by giving the content some personal experiences or advice.

Don't use unusual/experimental color combinations in your printed material. *A message needs to be clear* and the text is often better as black on a contrasting background.

Do try to use illustrations where you can and *gain permission for reproduction in writing* before going to print.

Don't be tempted to use any image with a less than print quality resolution at 300 dpi – *Downloads from the Internet are illegal and in breach of the rightful owner's copyright.*

5.21

GETTING THE STAFF TO START SELLING

Getting the staff to start selling

Where did the fear of sales & selling come from?

Whatever our opinions and views on sales might be, it is at the very center of our industry. We can try and ignore it in the hope that it will go away, but eventually like the tide it will catch up with you and then it's *sink or swim!* As trained professionals, we all know and can see the benefits of selling. **Yet for some it's fine, as long as they don't have to do it.** This way of thinking has to change as there is no longer a place for it in the salons and businesses of today.

The attitude towards retail sales in the hair salon or spa is often challenging, and many salon owners struggle to find ways to motivate their staff; so that they embrace the principles of selling to their clients. Most stylists would cringe at the idea of being employed as *'salespeople'* and really struggle with the fact that retail sales are a key part of the salon services that they **must** provide.

In this chapter, we consider some of the challenges and issues confronting both you and your staff and provide an insight in how to find a more balanced approach. In order to find a lasting solution to these problems, everyone should be ready, willing, and able to change their outlook and perception of selling and sales in the future.

People are *'creatures of routine'* and will naturally resist change, so the best way to manage in an ever-changing world, is to stop people developing routines in the first place. *(Or even better; make sure that the adopted routines incorporate selling from the outset.)*

Training is key and ideally, the change has to start when young trainees are taught client consultation. Inexperienced staff need to learn that products go *'hand-in-hand'* with the services they provide and an easy solution for their clients in the longer-term.

Remember that clients will always want to achieve similar effects to that of their stylist and professional products play an important part of the solution. So, with this in mind - it becomes part of the standard service and should form an integral part of any salon's service policy.

Sadly, a *malaise* has crept in, which condones the stylist's often lazy approach to retail sales, and many have avoided getting involved altogether. This has created a salon *'hit'* or *'miss'* policy and allowed those who feel comfortable selling, to do it - *and those who cannot be bothered to just 'get by' on the poor level of service that they always deliver!*

There should be no *hiding-place* for the salons and spas that represent a complacent, unprofessional business model. Poor service is a thing of the past and a *passport* to an inevitable failure!

"I would like to bring this to your attention now as in my experience, the table below highlights the main factors surrounding 'missed sales' opportunities and the reasons for poor staff performance."

Factors affecting poor retail sales	
Poor attitudes	Why / how has this negativity been allowed to develop? Who should intervene and at what point?
Lack of training	Why / how has this fundamental aspect been missed out?
Poor salon support	Who should be approached – how can the manufacturer help?
Fear due to poor knowledge	How can a stylist lack confidence – have they missed something during training?
Wrong 'fit' for job role	Poor appraisal, no job description, no clear targets or objectives

6.02

STOP!!!

Think about the following for a moment.

Q. Why do you use the particular ranges of products that you do for styling, coloring, perming, relaxing, hair-ups, extensions, etc.?

When you arrive at your best answer, you will have covered the following.

☑ *"I like the way that the products work."*
☑ *"I like the results that they provide."*
☑ *"I rely on them to do a job efficiently & effectively."*
☑ *"They suit my budget."*

You are *sold* on their features and benefits.

So, all you need to do now, is 'pass-on' that same passion and belief to your staff and clients.

When we think about sales and selling, we often consider them to be the same thing.

So what is selling?

Are sales & selling really that different?

Look at the two following examples:

Sales.

This could be the number of services that a stylist has performed either daily or weekly. The amount of services relates directly to a financial figure based on the salon's pricing. Additional sales can be achieved by *'up-selling'* i.e. recommending add-on services and treatments. Typically, this would occur when a client comes in for a new look or style then during the consultation the hair stylist recommends a different styling service e.g. color or highlights, and this is known as *up-selling*. This does produce a greater financial return but works on the principle that the client had already committed to purchasing anyway.

Selling

Selling is about making sales to people who had no previous intention of making a purchase. Therefore, this type of sale is potentially more difficult than just improving existing sales.

> ▸ *So why is selling seen as such an issue to stylists?*

> ▸ *Why are the sales of retail products an issue to the salon owner?*

There is a general misconception held by many salons operatives -

> ▸ *They feel that retail selling is below them*

> ▸ *It somehow cheapens who they are and what they perceive themselves to be*

> ▸ *They feel that it somehow diminishes their professional standing as a trained, creative hair stylist.*

They consider that someone else should handle retail sales and that normally refers to the receptionist.

How important is retail to a salon?

It has the following effects:

▷ *Significant financial benefits*

▷ *Provides attractive displays*

▷ *Provides incentives to earn more*

▷ *Compliments the salon's services*

A salon owner will see retail sales as another, alternative, revenue for the salon. It also enhances the services that the salon provides to its customers. It enables the client to purchase useful products that will help with their particular needs and extend the salon service as part of a planned home maintenance/care regimen.

Retail may be difficult to start with, but when staff are familiar to the concepts, it provides a self-perpetuating income and revenue stream to the business. The salons that are successful in building a strong retail business and a team who willingly support it, will achieve impressive retail sales figures.

Remember - the success can be measured in two ways.

▶ Increased salon profitability

▶ Opportunities for staff to earn more

The value of retailing in a salon

Retail does provide new opportunities for everyone, but first and foremost, you have to remember that *every* client is different, and each have individual needs. If you lose sight of your customer's needs and try to apply a 'one size fits all' rationale to your retailing, it will definitely fail. If you want to raise your earnings potential by introducing retail products, you need to ensure that your ranges are comprehensive enough to meet the needs of your salon's clientèle.

Remember, if they do not receive any personal advice and do not purchase the products that they need from the salon, they will go elsewhere, or shop online!

All the staff need to understand that retail sales are mutually beneficial to the business and that everyone benefits by taking part. The salon buys products and sells them to generate additional income. Without those extra margins, it would be unlikely that there would be any manoeuvrability at all, for enhancing the staff's salaries.

Staff need to remember that at least half of any professional consultation is about **giving good advice** and that they are doing their clients a disservice if they fail to inform them about how they can maintain their own hair at home, between salon visits.

126

The benefits of retailing:

From the salon's stand-point

- ☑ Increased sales / increased profits

- ☑ It provides more 'clout' i.e. an ability to negotiate even better deals

- ☑ Normally provides most backwash items as part of the 'intro' arrangements

- ☑ Raises salon profile and public awareness

- ☑ Increases salon's earnings potentials

- ☑ Provides 'one-stop' shopping options and enhances the salon's service offering

From the stylist's stand-point

- ☑ It becomes a routine aspect of the day-to-day job

- ☑ Increases staff earnings potentials

- ☑ Enhances professional standing/status, raises public awareness

- ☑ Greater client respect helps to build professional relationships

- ☑ Provides learning and self-development opportunities

From the client's standpoint

- ☑ Improves service experience

- ☑ Adds value and professionalism

- ☑ Provides a personalized service with individual attention

- ☑ Feel good factor

6.04

Income & Profitability
facts & myths

As a *footnote* to the points raised earlier, it is worth remembering that there are very few options for increasing salon sales and profit margins.

Other than retailing, you can only generate higher annual sales by:

- ▸ Employing more staff

- ▸ Encouraging clients to return earlier than your normal pattern of repeat

- ▸ Finding more clients

- ▸ Working longer hours

- ▸ Raising your prices

Employing more staff

It is a consideration, but the majority of salons are already complaining that they can't find suitable staff. It may be easier to be more effective with the ones that you have.

Encouraging clients to return sooner

You can increase sales significantly if you can get clients to return just one week earlier than normal. A client that returns on a five weekly basis, (rather than six), will contribute an additional 18% increase on your annual income. If you factor this across the business, it will provide some excellent returns. *But remember, all of the clients would need to return earlier, not just a few.*

Find more clients

It's not impossible, everyone needs to increase their clientèle to cover for clients moving away for new jobs, different lifestyles education, etc. But it is harder when all the competition are looking for new clients as well!

Working longer hours

It is possible to extend hours, and this is one way of finding new clients who would not be able to come at any other times. However, most salons are already overextended on hours and finding the staff to work them is also another major consideration.

Raising your prices

You do need to increase prices from time to time to be *in-line* with inflation and wages anyway, but be careful not to price yourself out of the market. Keep an eye on your competition, because they are keeping an eye on you!

Keen salesperson vs reticent sceptic

Have you ever wondered why a client chooses to purchase from you rather than the local store? It is because of your recommendation. The client values your professional opinion because they trust you and your ability to do a good job.

Fact or fiction?

A big concern to stylist is recommending products that their clients can find cheaper elsewhere. Salons need to be aware of this and try to stay competitive.

Salon products are often of a better quality	**Fact**
All salon products are of equal quality	**Myth**
Organic and herbal labelling is best	**Myth**
Quality professional products will, over time improve the condition	**Fact**
Good quality hair products will help with color retention	**Fact**
The more expensive it is, the better it is	**Myth**
Professional products are designed for specific hair types	**Fact**

6.06

How keen is keen?
What is a reticent sceptic?

Is this fear, lack of knowledge, or laziness? There is a big difference between being keen and being over zealous.

Keenness is demonstrated by showing your willingness to offer sound technical advice, being able to recommend without being *pushy* or overpowering. It is about having the confidence to discuss a client's needs offering advice to them from a professional position of knowledge and user experience.

Reticence, on the other hand, is quite disconcerting. When a stylist's attitude manifests itself as fear, or laziness it can often be masking an inner weakness. These outward expressions are usually covering a lack of knowledge.

In order to have knowledge - one needs to be willing to learn and although studying does not come easily to everyone; having a willingness to learn is all that is required. Some people find it difficult to learn or retain information, and this inner fear will often *sound* like skepticism.

If you struggle with retaining information ask for help, don't let this hold you back from being a true professional. You can do it; there are many ways to learn, and there are ways that things can be explained, and this relates to the ways that you will be able to explain products to your clients. It

129

should not be complicated, and it should not hold you back.

"I would like to add thoughts for those staff members who are lazy and cannot be bothered, or who are generally sceptical. Perhaps they should be considering their options, or are you doing that for them? If they are not the 'right fit' for your salon's team, do you really need them? "

True team members should be sharing the same salon vision: - The values that you stand for and uphold along with the policy aspects that the others are following.

It's not the role of the stylist to question the salon owner's decisions, marketing plans or any strategy for taking the salon forwards. It is their role to be a team player support salon policy and be an 'ambassador' for what the salon offers and represents.

Product knowledge & awareness

▶ What does it mean?

▶ How much knowledge is required?

▶ Does it enhance the service?

▶ Does it help retail sales?

The principles of selling as part of a service

Key points to remember

➤ It's not about selling - it is professional advice and recommendation

➤ Believe in the products - trust them to do their job

➤ Use the products - demonstrate that they work for specific purposes

➤ Explain the features and benefits - clients need reassurance that they meet their particular needs

Techniques for selling products

➤ Recommendation - introduced during consultation - informing the client that there are products that will meet their needs

➤ Experiential - the physical experience gained through handling/holding touching and smelling

➤ Professional demonstration - use the products as part of the treatment or service

6.07

What does it mean?

True product knowledge is about knowing how particular ranges of products work and how they benefit particular hair and skin types. It is about being able to take this knowledge and use it to explain to our clients the benefits of specific products so they can make an informed choice and decision in regard to purchasing.

How much knowledge is required?

A good all round basic knowledge is all that is required for any team of stylists; this is what they *build* into their consultation and make as a routine part of their general advice. *Is there such a thing as too much knowledge? Yes,* there is no point *banging on* about technicalities or scientific formulations as the majority of people will be bored by the presentation. Only a small percentage of people are impressed by expert technical knowledge, the majority see it as 'showing-off', and that is a big barrier to any sales. Always make this clear with staff during product training and *unless they really know their client*, leave the technical info out.

For those clients who are particularly interested in a deeper understanding of *silicon, sulfates, parabens,* or *biodegradability* and *toxicity*. Make sure that the staff 'stick' to the manufacturer's product profiles and not some *pseudo-science* that has been assumed by watching TV adverts, or chemistry taken out of context.

"I can give you an example where I made this mistake with a client who was a surgeon. I was extolling the benefits of one particular treatment that had a patented formulation. During the conversation, I said that the product contained 'ceramide', and the client said; **"You're not putting that on my hair."** I asked why not and her reply was; "We use it 'in-theatre' as a bacterial sterilizer to clean down surgical equipment!"*

Does it enhance the service?

Yes, every time. Clients expect advice as part of the service that they are paying for. How many clients visit your salon and make no attempt to engage in conversation with their stylist? It is a routine part of every visit and within that appointment, the client will expect a certain amount of non-specific, *idle chit-chat*, but not all of it to be focused upon holidays, families and friends. There is more to hairstyling than that!

The stylist is the professional service provider, and the client is the paying customer. The advice received by the client improves the professional's *standing* and only goes to help *market* the business further afield when being talked about in other social circles.

Does it help retail sales?

Yes, recommendation works as a sales technique; it works in the same way, that it does when to friends talk together and recommend something that they have experienced. But remember – recommendation is a suggestion, it may be professional advice, but it's the client's choice and decision. - We have to accept that not every client will buy from us - *but they have to buy from somewhere.*

Touch, look, feel, ask questions, but **always** recommend

Our main aim when discussing products with our clients is to maintain a **professional service provider - customer** relationship. When that level of trust is established, it will lead to them taking our advice.

Remember, it's not about selling, it is about relationship building, - being able to share information through communication.

Being professional

The type and nature of our relationship that we develop with our client has a direct impact in the way that communicate with them. If we start out with an informal, casual approach with new clients, we are definitely sending the wrong message and will only make it more difficult for us in the longer run. However, if we strike the correct balance from the outset and set the relationship on a professional level, it makes our job a lot easier.

....

Anyone working in a personal service industry is put in a position of trust. That loyalty and any subsequent, or incidental sales are dependent upon that professional bond. We must never become complacent about our role as a service provider, or abuse our position and status.

....

How to spot sales opportunities during consultation

Consultation is the key to both salon and stylist success.

You must have a consultation formula that works for you, and it is vitally important to the professional service provider and client relationship. It may sound very repetitive, but having your own tried and tested consultation must facilitate the following:

▶ Client questions

▶ Actively listening

▶ Time to consider options

▶ Appropriate courses of action

The *art* of great consultation is a balance between, listening to the client, finding out what they need and asking the right questions. It is about listening and then being able to offer advice and creative solutions to practical problems.

The relationship that the stylist develops with their client in hairdressing is unique throughout the personal service sector. The trust that the client '*gifts*' to their stylist is not to be taken lightly, and all information should always be kept private and in the strictest confidence.

Questions & events that lead to sales opportunities

➤ How have they coped with the style between visits?

➤ What are their hair issues that need to be addressed?

➤ What styling products are they currently using - are they working?

➤ What is the planned service - does it need any particular care or maintenance?

➤ How does the client intend to maintain the look between salon visits?

6.08

Remember, *never break the clients' loyalty or trust through your idle gossip.*

What are the right questions to ask?

Every part of the consultation is an opportunity to learn something about the client.

Things to consider.

▸ Are they a *new* or *returning* client?

▸ Do you keep client records? If not. Why not? If yes, are they up-to-date?

▸ If *new* - try to get the full history of services and products

▸ If *returning* - be prepared, access their records before they arrive

Good housekeeping with client records is essential; it helps as reminders, prompts and often '*sets the scene*' for the next visit. It enables the stylist to pick-up where they left off.

....

For example, it could relate to a complimentary treatment that your client sampled, and this provides you with an opportunity to follow that up during the next visit.

....

....

Alternatively, it could be used for making brief notes, (although you will need to be careful what you record and how you keep that information secure.)

....

Most salons *(unless they have a designated receptionist)* are very poor at maintaining detailed client information and barely manage to maintain the minimum of essentials.

Typically, this would cover:

▸ Client service history

▸ Techniques used

▸ Dates and times

▸ Retail product sales

"Is that really enough? No, your salon policy should expect all the staff to be responsible for their own clients goodwill and hair needs. It should be part of their job description - let's face it - your business depends upon it!"

Factors supporting sales:

☑ Recommendation, offer a solution to a problem	Always produces satisfied clients
☑ All clients buy hair products from somewhere	Most clients use at least 3 products. Shampooing, conditioning and styling
☑ Focus upon individual client needs	Communication. Ask questions, provide answers, 'steer' the conversation gain opinions or views
☑ Client observations of professional products	Notice what your client sees. What are they looking at? Do they pick the product up to find out more?
☑ Your clients' experiences	*"My colour lasted longer. I find it easier to keep and look good most of the time. The supermarket products don't seem to get the same results."*
☑ Listen to your client's issues and concerns	Offer sound honest advice - recommend products that will help

6.09

Develop a sales synergy for salon services & retail products

Points to promote & focus upon

When discussing the features and benefits of retail products, the stylist should be promoting the merits of *professional hair products costing less in the long run.*

The quality of the ingredients - the concentration of active elements, the consistency, these are all features that contribute to the price differences to other inferior brands, or cheaper copies and alternatives. *(This is proven in many trade sectors where you find professional 'trade quality' items deliver the right results more effectively.)*

The amount of product required - is always less with quality products. The professional formulation should enable a client to use less and not have to repeat so often. These savings do add up over time, making professional products real value for money, and this should be reinforced and preferably demonstrated during the appointment.

With such a wide diversity of hair products on the market being supported by advertising and clever promotion. For example, on TV, the Internet and in magazines and celebrity endorsements, etc. It is essential that the stylist includes and uses all of the above information to educate their clients about the value of professional products.

Selling shared values & your salon vision

▶ *A salon ethos*

▶ *A collaborative approach to sales and recommendation*

So much has changed within our industry over the past twenty years, and further change is still to come. Initially, there was a shift away from the traditional model of 'in-salon' training; which created a constant supply of new talent coming up through the ranks.

With this, came a degree of loyalty, as both parties had a personal investment in the *one-to-one* training and the prospects of an ongoing professional career.

Admittedly, there were some staff loses as trainees became demotivated or lost the commitment to carry on, but this is only mirrored by the poor retention rates in the college/further educational system of today.

In both cases; even after qualification, there is still a relatively high drop-out through disillusionment, alternative career paths, or where young newly trained stylists find it hard to find jobs or progress elsewhere within the industry.

In principle, the apprenticeship model provides the best introduction into the hairdressing, and that is because the 'hands-on' experience and the spontaneity of real situations cannot be simulated. It provides the only *realistic working environment* and exposes the trainee to a client and service provider relationship from day one. However, even with this enhanced opportunity to learn, we still find that staff are more mobile and tend to move about to seek out the best deal whilst thinking that the *"Grass is always greener...."*

You cannot stop people wishing to better themselves or trying to improve their professional C.V., it's a natural progression, but always leave the door open and the room for negotiation. You never know, they may be back and sooner than you think!

You can only lead by example, and that should be built around a vision.

Remember, your goal should be aiming towards the creation of the environment that encourages the building of mutual, respectful, relationships and promotes opportunities to nurture and develop a culture of loyalty.

Good salon owners will always 'lead by example'. *The don't do as I do, do as I say* approach to business management just doesn't work anymore, particularly with teams working in small, *close-knit* groups. Leading by example has a far greater impact on smaller, more dynamic teams, so spend more time building the right team of like-minded people, do not settle for second best.

Remember, as a business manager; making an investment in the business is all about investing in people in the first place.

Most people have heard the saying: *"A problem shared is a problem halved."*

Well, it also follows that your vision for the business will not get off-the-ground unless you take the time to share it and explain it to the team.

It may sound rather *blunt,* but a good hairdressing business is built solely on its reputation. Good service and happy clients are the fundamental starting point and a theme, or thread that continues throughout the lifespan of the business. When good service stops, the business will too. You are the only person that can monitor and ensure that the positive theme continues and the only person responsible for ensuring that others respect it and honor it too!

A salon brand, which has a strong collaborative team spirit, develops a work culture that attracts other stylists like a *magnet*. If you want to succeed in recruiting the right staff for your team, then you look for people who want to aspire to be part of something that is good and positive. This business concept is the basis for developing a culture of learning, where caring and creativity is held within the environment that rewards excellence and professionalism.

Salon owners need to take more responsibility when it comes to the level of service they want to see delivered in their salons. Stylists need to have a more professional approach to work, their work-ethics and what *real* service means and that is having a greater respect for the clients.

Provide support information & educational material

The primary form of communication in any salon setting is oral. Good hair stylists are natural communicators, they find it easy to talk to people and make them feel at ease when they first meet them. During the consultation, they are sensitive to the client's feelings and careful how they find out all the things that they need to know. (*Before making an informed opinion*) At all points through the consultation, they are asking questions, listening to responses and acting upon the information they have been given.

This may be enough for experienced hair stylists, but generally, speaking it is not enough. We want our clients to be able to reflect on what we are presenting, and this is only possible if they have something that they can take away to digest at some other time.

At this point, every professional communicator should be looking for something that reinforces what they have been saying in a clear, unambiguous way. **Manufacturers are the best source for any printed support material.**

Written materials

Where possible; always use professionally produced pamphlets, leaflets and brochures, as these will be able to support your sales with focused, customer friendly information.

Create the right environment: - The retail display area

This section provides some brief notes for developing the right sales environment. For more detailed information *See Chapter 5 (pgs 93-120)*

▶ A comprehensive range of styling or treatment products

The extent of product ranges depends upon your level of investment. *Don't try to be "All things to all people"* Focus upon one or more hair product areas and cover a wide variety of options within that product range

▶ The products that you sell should reflect the image and *target market* of the salon

It is always useful to provide a varying of pricing options but remember, the products should be a true reflection of your target market and not be unrealistic. (I.e. a vanity, or status issue)

▶ Product position, promotion and display

The placement of your products and supporting display material is vitally important. Think about your customer and the experience that they will have when entering the salon and receiving salon services.

Reception and salon frontage will always be the main focal point - clients have to pass through this area when arriving and again when leaving.

Salon floor and work areas people like activity for many reasons. Use the salon work areas as promotional and display zones – ensure that products are available for handling (people gain a better experience when they are allowed to pick things up and handle them – the supermarket approach to selling)

6.12a

Create the right environment: - The retail display area

▶ Product knowledge – advice and recommendation

Good, general background knowledge of products is essential. Focus your knowledge on product benefits and be ready to give advice and answer technical questions

▶ Updates and recent developments

Regular team meetings are essential for sharing thoughts on products, discussing customer feedback and providing updates on promotional campaigns and product developments

Create the right environment: - Presentation

▶ Product ambassadors

Consider having a salon *"go-to"* person, someone who is the (manufacturer) trained salon product expert. Provides a good back-up and sales support system for less experienced/ confident staff

▶ Role plays and simulation

Practice *mini product* presentations at team meetings get all staff to take part in introducing a product and talking about it. Extend the mini-presentations by encouraging team feedback and question and answer sessions

▶ In-salon training days

Make sure that you set aside specific days/evenings within the calendar for staff development sessions.

Arrange for your manufacturers to run product knowledge classes 2 or 3 times a year and when new products come into the salon.

6.12b

Good & bad sales techniques

Good techniques:

▶ Listening	Hearing the client – allowing them to speak – listening to their hair requirements / concerns / needs
▶ Positive communication	Using the correct body language / terminology / manner and tone
▶ Acting and advising on information received	Responding to what you hear – basing your advice upon the clients' identified requirements
▶ Honesty	Basing your recommendations on the salon's product range's actual features and benefits
▶ Educate through knowledge	Provide advice to clients in a way that they will understand
▶ Confidence	Be confident in your approach with the client, take control of the consultation and work through the process in a logical sequence
▶ Provide advice	Use suggestion and consideration as your sales technique. It is far better being forcing; - "well that's my opinion, take it, or leave it."

Focus upon the good sales techniques, these can be developed over time for any level of experience. A stylist has to be honest about their abilities, their strengths and weaknesses. Focus upon on those areas that need some improvement and bring these in, as aims and objectives within appraisals

6.13a

Good & bad sales techniques

Bad techniques:

▶ Being pushy	Don't try to bully clients into buying your products, it may work once, but there will be no further repeat sales and the professional bond of loyalty will be broken
▶ Poor communication skills	Doing all the talking – not listening to the client
▶ Over confident ▶ Using technical terms or jargon	Knowing your products is one thing but trying to impress clients by using that knowledge in the wrong ways will expose you as a 'know-it-all' and may come over as patronizing or humiliating.
▶ Lack knowledge	Don't try to 'bluff' your way through consultation expressing false claims just because you haven't bothered to learn about the products that you sell.
▶ Uncaring attitude	Be sensitive to your client's requirements; try to show empathy by putting yourself in their position. That way you can *feel* how they feel about their hair
▶ Not asking the right questions ▶ Not acting on the information given ▶ Not responding to issues or concerns raised	Trying to manipulate the discussion by ignoring what you have heard and turning it around to what you want to say shows your contempt for the client and their feelings. It is a ruthless sales tactic that you would expect from direct sales, not from a professional & client scenario

6.13b

Support materials should be made available for:

▶ Stylists

▶ Clients

Often these pamphlets or brochures can be used to open up discussions, introduce the products, creating an ideal ice-breaker. The client needs support and courtesy; they need to feel that you know what you are talking about and not just *'spieling'* because you have been told to.

Remember, it is important that all staff are all familiar with any new information that can be used to support product sales.

Always approach your supplier for technical details for any of their products. It is easier to check that your written product information is correct before printing and could save you a lot of time and wasted money, particularly if your information is incorrect. You might find that they will be able to give you 'straight quotes' that you can use and images that can be reproduced.

Always be aware of how much interest your client is showing, if they start to switch-off then you may have lost them at some point, or they are not interested in what you are trying to sell.

Remember they do not want or need a product's ingredient list, formulation, or chemical breakdown, and they certainly do not want a science lesson!

A regular client is far more trusting than a new client, and the professional bond is much closer. This should not deter a stylist from promoting the salon's products to new clients; on the contrary, it provides an opportunity to set the relationship on a professional service provider - client basis from the outset.

*Remember, price is usually a key consideration for the client, **but never make assumptions about what they can, or can't afford.** This is a common mistake that many staff can make when they 'feel' that they know a client well. The client is always in control of their budgetary considerations and must make their own choices, based upon the information that they receive.*

What do clients need to know?

▶ How much does it cost?

Cost is not necessarily the first thing that they need to know, but it does generally rank quite high in the order of things discussed.

If you leave pricing to the end of your consultation it can be seen as a defensive action, therefore it can be introduced in the following way:

"This product *XYZ* priced at 14.95 is ideally suited to your particular hair type and condition **because**......"

▶ What does the product do – how will it benefit them, expected signs of improvement etc.

▶ How much to use or apply?

▶ How long will it last

This is the primary information - the focus for creating a sale. -This is vitally important to the client and is the advisory aspect that has links to;

➤ Their particular needs
➤ Cost savings /benefits
➤ Unique personal advise based upon professional knowledge

This is secondary information that is useful but provided after, to support the sales argument

➤ Formulation may be interesting to clients it may 'chime' with their personal lifestyle values and beliefs (e.g. Green issues, animal testing)

▶ Herbal /organic/ingredients

▶ Allergy tested

▶ Scent / perfume

➤ Skin sensitivities are very common and allergen information is particularly popular for families and children or clients who have had repeated chemical treatments

➤ Fragrance is a key sales feature and enhancement of a product, as this enable the client to gain further sensual experiences of a product (e.g. Strong ammonia / alkaline smells have always been a turn off for clients who have color or perm. *(This has prompted the advertising campaigns of 'No Ammonia')*

6.15

143

Providing incentives: rewarding & acknowledging excellence

There are many ways to reward staff and provide further incentives.

You can provide:

▸ Salary bonus, commission targets

▸ Education fund, perhaps with external training courses

▸ Tools and equipment

▸ In-salon competitions with prizes

Financial: cash commission targets

This chapter has looked at the different ways to improve the salon's income through retail sales. There are many other ways, but they all stem from the same fundamental starting point.

In order to inspire people to be more productive in their work, you have to be ready to invest your money in return. This is a common system in the hair and beauty business called commission, and it has widely been accepted as making up a large part of a stylist's salary.

The hair and beauty industry has always been focused upon; sales, financial targets commission, and cash incentives, and '*On Target Earnings*' **(OTE)**.

With businesses constantly trying to stay ahead of their competition, there is continual 'tweaking' of commission structures and bonus schemes. It would, however, be foolish to try and cover them all within this text because each type of promotion will create another type of incentive.

Business owners are always looking for new ways to offer different *stimuli*, whilst their employees are always looking for better enhancements for their total job package. This has always been a widely discussed topic, and the business has to consider all the running costs that go on behind the scenes, in order to create a viable scheme.

Remember, a stylist will always know what their financial contribution is to the salon, even if they do not have the business acumen to work out, or realize what a reasonable return should be. (i.e. as a reward for their hard efforts)

Therefore, anyone, who is challenged with designing a commission scheme, must consider the following factors:

▸ Actual turnover - potential turnover

▸ Staff contributions - potential contributions

▸ Amounts of new clients/customers

▸ Services provided - Products sold

▸ Client retention rates - size of clientèle

▸ Employee's length of service

▸ Labor costs - fixed costs

▸ Cost of consumables

All of these contribute to any decision made for an offer of bonus or commission rate or scale. If an employer wants to consider what their hairstylists (*rightly or wrongly*) are thinking. They might also think about the following **key performance indicators (*KPIs*)** as a way to add incentives for their staff.

What are the staff thinking about?

▸ Their total number of clients

▸ The number of services they provide in a shift/day/week, etc.

▸ The number of advance bookings / re-bookings they have

▸ Their total financial contribution to the business in relation to salary/ wages earned

▸ How valuable they are to the business

There is a balance to be found between the salon and stylist. However, it must be said that the cost of doing business is much higher than most stylists ever realize. It should also be considered that making more money and just being motivated by money and earnings can be very destructive and create a lot of negativity within a team.

Remember, if your only focus is doing and 'fitting-in' more people, (in an effort to bring in more money to reach a higher target,) you will start to take shortcuts and compromise the quality of your service.

Commissions have to be transparent and seen as fair, realistic, and achievable to all. However, where staff cannot see the business's standpoint, some explanation may be required. (If only to dispel the myth of *'rich and greedy'* salon owners.)

Remember, you are the businessperson and you cannot expect your staff to understand the difference between making a profit or a loss. Many employees will never understand the mathematical complexity of making the 'business' ends meet.

What are the best incentives to get a team motivated?

Pooling funds for education - courses, or seminars

Courses and seminars are always a great incentive, especially if the salon is progressive and inspiring. It's a *win-win* formula. If the salon thrives on doing exciting work, then what is better than making the training and continuing development of those skills, the reward for achieving the target?

Create an education fund that can be used for individual training or the salon team. This can be set up quite simply with a variety of manufacturers or specialist artistic groups and has the same impact and *magnetism* as that of 'cash' incentives.

Remember, anything saved and put towards staff development is a valid business cost, so any costs incurred such as course fees, transportation, accommodation and meals are tax deductible. This type of fund can either be set up as an incentive for individual business targets or focused upon the whole team's achievements.

Tools & equipment

A similar fund can be allocated for the purchase of personal equipment / tools. This can be of great help to a stylist who may want to upgrade or replace their shears / scissors, or particularly helpful if they are *cherished* items that they could never afford. Alternatively, it could be used as a way of expanding and developing new service areas that the team has identified. For example, starter kits, which are often a large initial outlay, say for ornamentation for hair-ups, or hair extensions, or perhaps a new coloring system.

Remember, if you did choose to offer these types of incentives, the business would need to cover its investment, and this may be something that would need to be covered contractually. Particularly if a member of staff were to leave prematurely and that investment in their future was lost to another competitor!

In-salon competition

These are always good for team building, and general morale and there are many types of competitions that can be arranged.

Manufacturers are very keen on this type of incentive and will often arrange a prize give-away, these can focus upon new product launches or promotions. They will prearrange with the salon a scale of incentives surrounding a product launch and provide the salon with all the necessary published information. Leaflets or brochures will focus upon the scale and range of prizes available and will also cover the timescales, terms and conditions. This can be distributed amongst the staff during routine staff meetings, and the competition can even involve the clients.

Healthy competition is seen as a positive motivator and is used by all businesses because people respond well to the chance of winning something. However, there are times and particularly with small, close-knit teams, that it can be a negative force.

If you think of sport, it is easy to see that many people are drawn towards running and racing, but there can only be one winner. Admittedly, there are also accolades for those coming in second and third, but what about the rest, what do they get out of it? It takes certain types of people that have the inner drive to pick themselves up and say. "I'm going to win next time." For many it is a case of "It's alright for Sarah, she always wins." In situations where this *is happening, the whole team will 'switch-off' to the incentives on offer and withdraw altogether.*

Alternatively, salons can arrange their own in-house competitions. For example, a salon **makeover** competition, this could involve the staff's friends and families, or clients. Local businesses could be approached to provide a panel of judges, and the local radio and newspaper could be invited to attend. It is a great way to help promote the business whilst giving an opportunity for your staff to get their name in the media.

Salon shows and competitions can be rewarding and the good publicity gained from being successful in regional or national heats in something like the *L'Oreal Colour Trophy* can be huge. However, this does take a lot of time and requires a mammoth team effort and a considerable business commitment. Many major competitions involve an initial photographic entry, and good artistic imagery and effects go way beyond the hairstyle!

'Deep pockets' or a little bit of luck?

We are all impressed by the quality of work that is produced each year for the *'catwalk'* collections of the *'Couture' Fashion* houses. Nevertheless, it is worth remembering that fashion photography is very expensive and *in order to be the best; you need the best.*

You may be lucky and know an aspiring photographer who is working their way to the *upper elite,* and they may be interested in working collaboratively on a variety of joint, artistic projects.

Where can I find help & support?

Our industry is diverse; it exists and extends to provide hairdressing services to all people regardless of age, race, status, income, demographics, or location. This creates a complex variety of considerations that cannot be addressed by a long list of websites. When we look closely at our clients' needs, we start to focus upon different types of customers, this has more to do with marketing than sales, and you will find out more about this topic in Chapter 2.

However, the list shown on the next page provides some useful links to a variety of higher level bodies responsible for the quality and delivery of recognized training and education.

Remember a little friendly competitiveness amongst team members is an incentive, whereas an over competitive 'gladiatorial' approach, where staff are pitched against each other is negative and works against the whole ethos of your customer service provision.

You are not trying to create a 'sales only' environment, but creating a business that is built on a good reputation. The biggest reward has to be a returning client who loves their hair - is recommending you. They trust your judgment, value your opinions and rely upon you for their appearance, hairstyle and product recommendations.

Additional sources for information can be found in *Appendix A pgs 167-169* at the back of this book.

Higher authorities – awarding organizations

▲ HABIA   Hair and Beauty Industry Authority www.habia.org   Responsible for identifying recognized standards within the industry

▲ City & Guilds   City & Guilds Institute of London www.cityandguilds.com   Providing information to industry about sources for training and education

▲ VTCT   Vocational Training Charitable Trust www.vtct.org.uk

▲ ITEC   ITEC World www.itecworld.co.uk   Awarding certification/ qualifications within the National Qualification Framework to candidates at approved centres

6.18

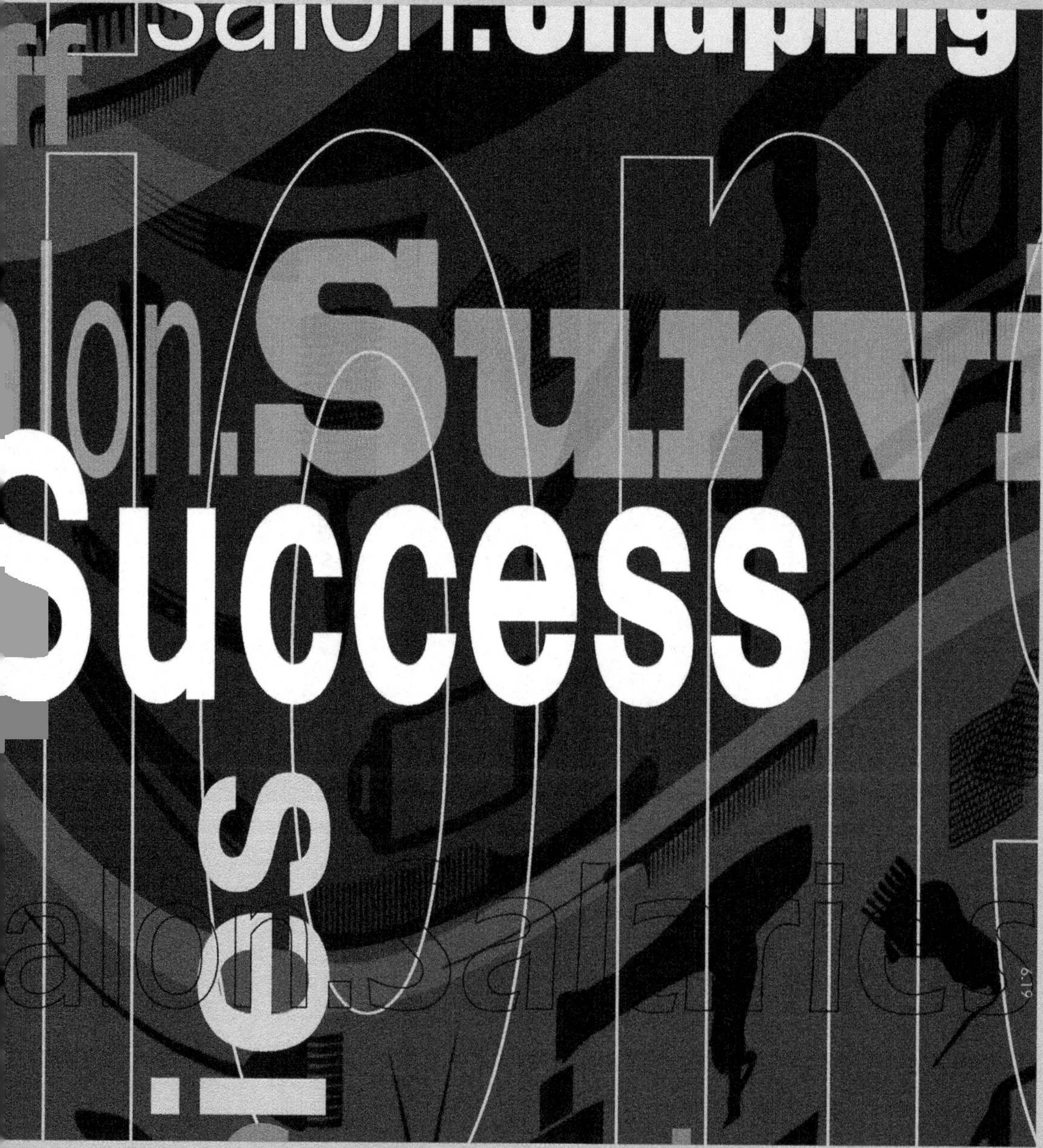
Success

7

FINAL THOUGHTS

Final thoughts

This final chapter provides us with an opportunity to review and reflect upon some of the areas we have covered. I hope that you will have found that there has been one common thread that has underpinned each of the topics and that has been good service. We all know that we are judged by our clients; on the quality of service we provide, but what does that really mean?

We have to measure quality of service in two different ways:

1. The level of skill that we use whilst providing services

2. The way in which we communicate whilst providing services

7.01

It may seem quite *glib* to reduce years of professional training and experience into two short statements, but we need to find ways to put all that energy and commitment into words that everyone can understand.

If we expand each of those statements, what do they mean in basic terms?

We know that the term skill refers to practical occupations, but how do we distinguish between the different levels of skill? If we are to believe the vocational qualification's definition, then we see that there are currently three different standards. These three different standards are measured by qualification, so let us assume that we have individuals who have completed each of the following:

Level 1

Level 1 relates to a novice, who has learned about some of the topics and duties relating to the craft and may be able to assist the stylists in their work. However, their limited skills would not allow them to complete technical services without supervision.

Level 2

Level 2 relates to a junior stylist who has completed a basic all-around training in a variety of hairdressing or barbering techniques. Whilst they acquired the technical skills, they also learned about the relevant basic science, health and safety and how to use products, tools and equipment to deliver the different technical services.

Level 3

Level 3 relating to a senior stylist who has developed their technical skills to a commercial level and may even specialize in some particular areas, e.g. advanced coloring techniques, hair ups, hair extensions, etc. A senior stylist with have good communication skills, be confident with clients and their needs and may even supervise the consultations undertaken by junior stylists.

First of all, we don't want to take anything away from those that have already achieved those standards but are they really enough to equip someone in our industry today?

The answer is quite simply NO. The clients of today demand and expect much more, and we need to find ways in which we can make this happen or get out of the business altogether.

Skill is a combination of things, and when someone acquires a skill they are able to carry out a sequence or process; i.e. 'method,' and then apply the knowledge they have learned about the task to the method, in order to do the process correctly. Therefore, hairdressing and barbering are vocations; craft based occupations that enable people to show different degrees of skill, not qualification.

Many people within the industry say that the current standards do not go far enough, why do you think that is? The main problem with most qualifications is that they are focused on people who want to enter into a particular industry/sector or be able to do so something.

Thinking along these lines, we could say that the qualification structure in hairdressing and barbering is front loaded and pressurizes those who enter the craft. It then leaves individuals in a sink or swim scenario; those who do well stay in it and progress, those that do not tend to leave or work on a temporary or part-time basis.

It seems quite cruel, but it is a tough occupation. It's a money problem, and anything related to education and training is costly. So unless an industry has the structure to collect funds to support it, and then it will flounder at anything past mainstream (government funded) education. Therefore, the main focus for our hair industry, targets these three qualifications for those between school leaving age and those in their early twenties. Unlike other professions, there is no ongoing system of continuing professional development.

Therefore, without any further levels of recognizable professional skills or qualifications, salaries tend to peak, then the only way to increase personal income, is through commissions and increased sales.

Sadly, this rush, to acquire qualifications quickly, has a negative impact on those who have significant experience. People thrive on achievement, so whilst they are busy striving to reach the next level, they are self-motivated and keen to do well. When the challenge disappears, the motivation tails off and people lose interest in their work. Hair styling was never intended to be routine or mundane; it is supposed to be exciting, so the only way, which the energy can reinvigorated, is if you make it happen.

What do you want to be running; a boring or exciting salon? The choice is yours.

Soft Skills

The advent of *'soft skills'* within the workplace may be the missing link. Until now the educational policy for our hair sector has looked at two different aspects of learning and uses the outcomes from these in order to make a judgement upon people's competence for completing a task successfully.

> ▸ **The first part of an assessment; made by observation, judges a person's ability to do a practical task**

> ▸ **The second part of the assessment; made by questioning, judges the person's knowledge and under-standing of things relating to the practical process**

If this were enough, then all assessment could be made on modelling heads as clients would not be needed!

Now we get closer to the problem, it is not just the way in which processes are done, or what we can profess to know that counts. It is more about how we communicate with our clients whilst all these other things are going on that matter. This is how we add value to the service part and make the difference between the services offered in one salon or another.

So what are soft skills?

Soft skills relate to the personal qualities and attributes that someone uses in order to succeed in their work. They cover a range of communication skills such as ability to listen well, to communicate effectively, being positive, managing conflict, accepting responsibility, showing respect, building trust, working well with others, managing their time effectively, accepting criticism, working under pressure, being likeable, and being able to demonstrate good manners.

If we were to create a profile for someone who might demonstrate these things in their work we could add; being trustworthy, having empathy, good work ethics, shows enthusiasm,is optimistic, has integrity,good motivation, is professional. Soft skills are relevant to all workers and employees in any occupation, at any level including management.

The following illustration shows how soft skills can be demonstrated in different work scenarios.

Soft Skills

Personal communication	Active listening	Pleasant, professional manner	Asking relevant/good questions
	Accurate communication	Clear written communication	Communicate correctly using social media
	Clear oral explanation, being understood		
Self-management skills	Self motivated	Sense of duty and urgency	Open to self-development opportunities
	Good work ethics, loyal	Work well under pressure	Adapt to different situations,
	Punctual, work to time		
Teamwork skills	Productive team member	Responsible team member	Openness to and with others
	Meets deadlines and targets	Accountable takes ownership of the task	Sharing ideas with others
	Positive, encouraging attitude	Applies different approaches to others and their work	

7.02a

155

Soft Skills cont.

Professionalism skills	Effective relationships with customers, business connections	Able to understand the needs of others	Manages own body language - non-verbal communication
	Accepts criticism and responds appropriately	Understands own role and career opportunities	Recognizes the needs of others through their body language – non-verbal communication
	Confidential, trustworthy with sensitive information		Select appropriate sources for information or advice
Decision making / problem solving skills	Identify and analyze problems	Creative with solutions	Evaluate effectiveness
	Take effective and appropriate action	Transfer knowledge to/in different situations	Interpret ideas, make comparisons
	Realize effect/ impact of decisions		7.02b

Product Survey 2014

Salonstudies conducted a survey during the latter part of 2014, and business professionals were asked to contribute by 'posting' their feedback on the website. The survey was open to all, and the bulk of the contributions were made by business owners, with some comments from the educational sector.

List of contributors – Salonstudies would like to thank the people listed below for their time and contribution to the survey.

People were asked to comment on hairdressing products of their choice and without any specific direction, this enabled people to talk about products that they liked as well as those that they felt had under-performed.

The purpose of the survey was to provide a system that shared published information from professionals who never really get the chance to make comparisons with their peers. Each submission was made by online *form* entry and contributors were asked to respond to specific questions.

We have published some of their feedback on the following pages, but a complete record of the survey is available on the *Salonstudies.com* website.

Louise Allen	Daron Griffiths
John Baker	Masaki Inoue
Kristina Blagus	Diane Kuhns
Mette Buchhave	Cathy Lehner
Erika Burban	Sal Logerfo
Jeanmarie Cestare	David Mackinnon
Siobhan Clark	Jacqui Marola
Shelley Dalton	Ken Moshier
Pam Decharo	Julie Rimmer
Jane DeFrancesco	Chris Rivera
Jason DiFato	Stewart Roberts
Donna Farrar	Gary Sunderland
Nanette Ferguson	Judie Tallman
Rachael Fleshman	Melony Terry
Darcy Fox	Jill Willcox
Jeni Giles	Daron Griffiths
Dawn Griffith	Masaki Inoue

Prod.	Mfg	Experience with this	Benefits	Rating	Reason
Wave it	Schwarzkopf	Great product for achieving a soft curl with no-frizz and fantastic condition afterwards. Gentle on the hair and a pleasant smell, unlike some permanent waves.	This product benefits hair as it has a gentle formulae that is easy to use; it leaves the hair in the same condition as beforehand.	5*	It does exactly what it says on the box. It waves the hair and gives body without compromising the texture and condition of the hair
Lemon Sage Thickening Shampoo	Paul Mitchell	Love this product as with most of the Paul Mitchell *Tea Tree* range It does what it says, smells nice and is economical if used as recommended	Thickens and Cleanses .. Smells nice and gives / leaves an invigorating feeling	5*	I've used this product for some time and it has never let me down. "It does what it says it does"
Diamond Oil	Redken	Client can feel the different after one use in salon. She automatically wanted to buy complete range for home use.	Hair is so soft,shiny , easy for brushing	5*	Product gives instant results and is easy to sell
Falengreen	Soulglow	Lovely to finally get a shampoo with no perfume and at the same time keeps my hair shiny and soft.		5*	

7.04a

158

Illumina color	**Wella**	This is the best color I have ever used. It is cool, throws no red. It can be applied from roots to ends with no banding and the hair is left in amazing condition. The longevity of the product is amazing and it does not fade nor does the reflect fade.		It truly is a new easier to use product that a junior can safely apply without worrying about banding. Finally a product for the client that wants no warmth at all in their color that does not look flat or have a green hue.
				5*
Top chic & Colorance	**Goldwell**	Goldwell is one of the most comprehensive lines available. Being a colorist I appreciate the fact that using your knowledge and their color, you can create anything you need to. The fact that they offer watch and learn classes online is very convenient to myself and my staff. THE BEST!!	The technology behind Goldwell always works on keeping the integrity of the hair. Through *intra-lipid* technology, hair is left in better condition after it's been colored. There is also less fading. Silk-Lift is conditioning while lightening. No other lightener works like it. BEAUTIFUL AND HEALTHY!!	Keeping the integrity of a clients hair as well as creating beautiful colors is very important. Goldwell allows you to do that using *Intra-Lipid* technology. They also offer an ammonia free permanent color that can also give 3 levels of lift. Truly the best option for a true colorist!
				5*
Trauma Treatment	**L'anza**	This is a great product for adding to color to help protect and nourish the hair in coloring, as a restorative treatment and component in the healing care line. By no means will they repair damage to the hair caused by overuse of heat etc but it does help protect further damage.	Versatile use with color. As a treatment and a conditioner. Affordable.	PH neutral, nourishes hair, prolongs color.
				5*
Brazilian Blow Dry	**Inoar**	Excellent product achieves results as described by the manufacturer. Easy to use and clients experience the wow factor.	Smooths, strengthens and decreases frizz. Can also be used to elongate curls for clients wanting to retain natural curl patterns.	Makes my hairdressing life easier and enables me to provide clients with hair textures that they didn't believe they could achieve.
				5*

159

Product	Brand				
Colorance	Goldwell	I think it's the best quality color available. I also like the way you can measure it out - less waste - and the results are always shiny, glossy and true to color. We also get a fair amount of training from Goldwell, which is significant.	The quality of the product is very high. Goldwell is loaded with buffers, and the bleaches are not as damaging as most as a result. The colors are so rich that they fade far less than normally seen.	5*	Having used many different high-end color lines, I have learned through experience that GW is the best. We used *Framesi* for many years, and the 2 lines DO compare, but I feel that GW is easier to use plus the colors last and are less damaging
Thrill	Schwarzkopf	A cream gel with a level 2 styling hold. Creates texture in the hair without over loading the hair shaft.	Gives body and hold to the hair and maintains shine, helps define texture	5*	Some other gels can leave the hair sticky and dull.
Fusion, Shades EQ	Redken	Professional, World exposure, Great education	Gentle formula, consistent results.	5*	Many choices for different results.
K-Pak	Joico	Total rebuild hair	The molecular weight allows it to go all the way down to the medula	5*	Results of it transforming hair
Igora Royal	Schwarzkopf	Know this product well, and like using it.	Gives required color.	4*	Easy to use and gives consistent results.

7.04c

160

7.04d

Product	Brand				
Blow Dry Spray	Scruples	This product delivers, creates shine, manageability and softness to the hair. A *must have* for every hair type	Because of the decreased blow drying time the hair remains healthier.	5*	When the product was introduced to me I was amazed at the performance. It delivered exactly what I was told.
Hair Color 'Shampoo & Conditioners	L'anza	Love the color line its flexibility love the fact I don't have to buy three lines to get what I want to achieve a color!!! Love the grey coverage, Love the grow out it looks so good!!! It does not have an awful smell as some color lines do!! I also like the hair product line as well.	I think it is great on the hair I actually have switched all my clients from Aveda to L'anza , Aveda was very drying and L'anza is very conditioning to hair. My clients hair feels and looks great!		
Blazing Hair Lowlights	Scruples	Easy to formulate and apply, some color choices seem to fade very warm or golden	Designed with contributing pigment bases factored in for tinting back over previously highlighted, lightened or bleached hair	5*	Some colors fade excessively warm or golden
Keratin Healing Oil	L'anza	Treats the hair whether using as a treatment, blow-dry oil or a finishing product. This is not a greasy or heavy product. Clients feel and see the difference immediately.	Colored hair reflects the colors, leaves hair smooth and feeling light. Is treating the hair so is long term beneficial.	5*	There are many hair oils in the professional market, this is the best one I have used to date. Delivering what it promises

Product	Brand	Description	Review	Rating	Final Thoughts
L'Kerabelle	L'Kerabelle	L'Kerabelle produces shampoos, conditioners, a treatment and styling products. They all contain both a complement of protein (Keratin) and moisture to keep hair healthy and help prolong the effect of the amazing K-Fusion Treatment	L'Kerabelle have developed a range of products that not only keep hair that has had a K-Fusion Treatment in the best of health, but actually helps prolong the life of a K-Fusion Treatment.	5*	I have had the good fortune, as a hairdresser, to have been involved with creation and ongoing development of L'Kerabelle and K-Fusion. I myself, hold very high standards with my work and the tools and products I use. With that said, I know L'Kerabelle uses only the finest ingredients available.
Sade Eq	Redken	Nicely toned shades with less damaging the chemically treated hair.	Conditions the hair while glazing the processes the hair	5*	I use them in the past and never disappointed. Many professionals agreed the same way;)
Top Chic	Goldwell	Love it! Canisters offer an accurate measuring system for precise and consistent outcome and prevents waste. Product stays fresh much longer in canisters versus a tube.	Great conditioning properties and adds lots of shine. Leaves hair in better condition than started with. Gives vibrant & rich color results every time.	5*	Never disappointed with the results I achieve.
Big Sexy Root Pump Plus	Aestelance	Big Sexy Root Pump Plus is by far my favorite styling product on earth. With a directed spray nozzle, one can target the areas that you want superior lift in when styling. It has a wonderful hold that is not sticky, crunchy or soft. Great for big hair or weekly styling	It makes it easy to get great moveable volume without drying out the hair	5*	I have been using this product for 20+ years in weekly styling as well as voluminous styles

7.04e

Product	Brand				
Lisclo Crystal Organic Cream	Milbon	I was the senior educator for this company for 5 years. I helped in the development of Crystal Cream. It is superior to any other on the market for straightening, smoothing and frizz removal with no harmful fumes!	Leaves the hair in beautiful condition,with an amazing shine,silky touch. The hair still has body and movement when a full thermal straightening is done.	5*	Many options to achieve the end result desired after the client consultation.from frizz removal,smoothing (more styling options) to full 'Japanese' Straightening.
EverEscents Organic	EverEscents	Highly effective does what is says it will do, organic, great price point and mark-up	Does the job	5*	No nasties large organic component
Keune tinta color	Keune	Best color I have used as it has a nice smell, leaves the hair in fab condition and the company is great to work with also has the added bonus of no PPDs	No alcohol,leaves the hair shinier, not so much scalp staining and less color fade	5*	All my team chose this over other color houses after we tested them, we all get on really well with Tinta as it leaves the hair in better condition,shinier and easy to work with great coverage
Frehair - Low PH Rinse	Mastey	I have used this product since the mid 70's. Frehair helps to eliminate tangles & is very lightweight which I love in a conditioner. It also is a great low PH rinse that eliminates static while 'locking in' your color.	Leaves hair tangle-free without weighing it down-Eliminates static electricity and fly-away hair-Leaves hair with appropriate wetness and comb-ability for in-salon cutting and styling	5*	Frehair smooths and softens the hair & leaves it shiny & ready for easy combing, brushing and styling Leaves hair tangle-free without weighing it down & eliminates static. Contains no oils, waxes or dyes.

163

Product	Brand			Rating	
Inoa	L'Oreal	Inoa uses an oil delivery system instead of ammonia to deposit color into the cortex of the hair. The condition of the hair is noticeably softer to touch and glossier. I find the colors true to shade and tone so there is no guess work,is easy to remove, for those who like to change color often.	Ammonia free- Reduction in swelling better for hair condition. Oil delivery system- replaces the action of ammonia. 100% grey coverage. Creamy consistency. True to shade and tone A wide variety of shades 60 ml tubes with 1+1 mixing ratio Color removes easily with color remover	5*	Add all the product benefits and innovative technology to my Excellent rating and in addition to that, its the first permanent hair color I have used a 9 level and 20 vol on a natural level 7 and not had a yellowish undertone. it looks like a natural 9 not a tinted 9.
All	Global Keratin	Love this product. It's easy to work with and it leaves the integrity of the hair in better shape than it started with.	It gives the hair a beautiful shine, makes it feel and look healthy. I start shy clients on it with just the fringe, so the can see how it works. They are always back for the full treatment, even those with short hair. Life is easy for them now	5*	It's all about the client. If I can help them make their hair dreams come true, great. It's such a great aid. Wear it wavy or wear it straight, versatility is the key, and healthy looking hair.
Anti-thining programme	L'Oreal	I have had fantastic results with this amazing product. I have had clients put on Facebook how much better their hair has been after only a week.	Makes the hair look and feel fuller with more body	5*	I have rated it excellent due to the in salon results I have witnessed along with client feedback we
Hocus Pocus	Hair Wizard	Excellent non aerosol styling mousse great for blow drying just pump into your hand work into the hair and start styling	Non aerosol hand pump mousse weightless yet adds volume natural product produced in the uk	5*	Works really well not sticky not smelly ideal for the stylists and the client nicely presented

7.04g

Sade Eq — Redken

Nicely tones shade with less damaging the chemically treated hair.

Conditions the hair while glazing the processed hair.

5*

I use them in the past and never disappointed. Many professional agreed the same way :)

7.04h

Hypnotic — Scruples

Excellent in filling and coloring hair in one step, one application. The color is formulated in such a way that you don't have to mess with figuring out what to fill the hair with first, no muddy colors and the hair looks and feels great after. Saves time, saves money too.

Hypnotic single step creme low lights leaves the hair looking and feeling healthy. Color is rich, not muddy Low ammonia conditioning color, enriched with acai berry, acacia flower extract, aloe Vera, avocado oil

5*

This product takes the time and guess work out of filling and coloring hair, leaves the hair in great condition, in the way the hair feels after color, also the time that is saved by not having to fill, wait, rinse, dry and then adding another color, and processing a second time.

Power lift — Redken

Excellent lifting action that does not expand a great deal. Gives you the option of high lift or ammonia free. The negative I have is that our supplier will not deliver it.

Choice of high lift or ammonia free. Creamy texture with out a lot of expansion.

5*

Trading Information

Please note that the following information is correct at the time of publication and that consumer legislation varies greatly between different countries. (And states or provinces if applicable.) We recommend that your first point of contact should be your local authorities and that the following information provides some additional sources and starting points.

....

United Kingdom:

Consumer Protection Act [1987]

This Act follows European laws to protect the buyer in the following areas:

> *Product liability* – a customer may claim compensation for a product that doesn't reach general standards of safety
> *General safety requirements* – it is a criminal offence to sell goods that are unsafe; traders that breach this conduct may face fines or even imprisonment
> *Misleading prices* – misleading consumers with wrongly displayed prices is also an offence.

The Act is designed to help safeguard the consumer from products that do not reach reasonable levels of safety. Your salon will take adequate precautions in procuring, using and supplying reputable products and maintaining them so that they remain in good condition.

Trade Descriptions Act [1968 & 1972]

Products must not be falsely or misleadingly described in relation to their quality, fitness, price or purpose, by advertisements, orally, displays or descriptions. And since 1972 it has also been a requirement to label a product clearly, so that the buyer can see where the product was made. Briefly, a retailer cannot:

> Mislead consumers by making false statements about products
> Offer sale products at half price unless they have been offered at the actual price for a reasonable length of time.

The Resale Prices Act [1964 & 1972]

The manufacturers can supply a recommended price (MRRP or manufacturers' recommended retail price), but the seller is not obliged to sell at the recommended price.

Trade Associations

British Association of Beauty Therapy and Cosetology Limited (BABTAC)
Ambrose House, Meteor Court, Barnett Way, Barnwood,
Gloucester GL4 3GG
Tel: 01452 623110
Fax: 01452 611599
www.babtac.com

Cosmetic, Toiletry and Perfumery Association (CTPA)
Josaron House, 5–7 John Princes Street, London W1G 0JN
Tel: 020 7491 8891
www.ctpa.org.uk
www.thefactsabout.co.uk

Fellowship for British Hairdressing
Bloxham Mill, Barford Road, Bloxham, Banbury, Oxfordshire
OX15 4FF
Tel: 01295 724579
www.fellowshiphair.com

Freelance Hair and Beauty Federation
FHBF Head Office, The Business Centre, Kimpton Road,
Luton, Bedfordshire LU2 0LB
www.fhbf.org.uk

The Hairdressing and Beauty Suppliers Association
Greenleaf House, 128 Darkes Lane, Potters Bar,
Hertfordshire EN6 1AE
Tel: 01707 649499
www.thehbsa.uk.com

The Hairdressing Council (HC)
30 Sydenham Road, Croydon, Surrey CR0 2EFT
Tel: 020 8771 6205
www.haircouncil.org.uk

Trade Associations (cont.)

Health and Beauty Employers Federation
(part of the Federation of Holistic Therapists)
18 Shakespeare Business Centre, Hathaway Close,
Eastleigh, Hampshire SO50 4SR
Tel: 023 8062 4350
www.fht.org.uk

Incorporated Guild of Hairdressers, Wigmakers
and Perfumers
Langdale Road, Barnsley, South Yorkshire S71 1AQ
Tel: 01226 786 555
Fax: 01226 731 814

National Hairdressers' Federation (NHF)
One Abbey Court, Fraser Road, Priory Business Park,
Bedford MK44 3WH
www.the-nhf.org
Tel: 01234 831965 or 0845 345 6500

Legal & Regulatory

Equality and Human Rights Commission (EHRC)
Equality Advisory Support Service
Tel: 0808 800 0082
www.equalityhumanrights.com

Health and Safety Executive
Publications:
PO Box 1999, Sudbury, Suffolk CO10 6FS
HSE Infoline:
Tel: 0845 345 0055
www.hse.gov.uk

Union of Shop, Distributive and Allied Workers (USDAW)
188 Wilmslow Road, Fallowfield, Manchester M14 6LJ
Tel: 0161 224 2804 / 249 2400

Trade Shows: UK

> http://www.salonexhibitions.co.uk

Australia:

Consumer Protection: State & Territory Consumer Protection Agencies

Your local state and territory consumer protection agency (sometimes called 'consumer affairs') can provide you with information about your rights and options. They may also be able to help negotiate a resolution between you and the seller.

> Australian Capital Territory
> New South Wales
> Northern Territory
> Queensland
> South Australia
> Tasmania
> Victoria
> Western Australia

For more information - contact small business helpline on. 1300 302 021.

The ACCC will answer your questions and provide information and services for you. Resources are available from the ACCC's websites and other government departments and organizations.

☑ http://www.accc.gov.au/business
☑ http://www.accc.gov.au/contact-us/other-helpful-agencies/state-territory-consumer-protection-agencies

Trade Shows: Australia

> http://www.reedexhibitions.com.au/events/hair-and-beauty/
> http://www.eventseye.com/fairs/f-hair-expo-australia-13135-1.html
> http://www.hairexpoaustralia.com
> http://hbia.com.au

Canada:

Consumer Affairs Industry Canada

➤ 235 Queen Street, 2nd Floor, West Tower Ottawa, Ontario K1A 0H5 Tel: (613) 946-2576 Fax: (613) 952-6927

Provincial and Territorial Consumer Affairs Offices

☑ http://www.consumerinformation.ca/eic/site/032.nsf/eng/01112.html - prov

☑ http://www.ic.gc.ca/eic/site/oca-bc.nsf/eng/home

ConsumerInformation.ca

ConsumerInformation.ca is Canada's most extensive source of online consumer information. It provides Canadian consumers with a single-source window to information and contacts for many consumer-related enquiries. The initiative is founded on a strategic partnership among federal departments and agencies, provincial and territorial ministries and non-government organizations.

For more information, visit

➤ www.ConsumerInformation.ca.

➤ http://www.tradecommissioner.gc.ca/eng/find-trade-contacts.jsp

Trade Shows: Canada

➤ http://www.abacanada.com

United States America

Federal Trade Commission

- 600 Pennsylvania Avenue, NW Washington, DC 20580 Telephone: (202) 326-2222
- Federal Trade Commission 400 7th St., SW Washington, DC 20024 Telephone: (202) 326-2222

Bureau of Consumer Protection

- Bureau of Consumer Protection Federal Trade Commission 600 Pennsylvania Ave., NW Washington, DC 20580

Trade Associations:

- http://www.beautyweb.com/beauty_associations.htm

Trade Shows: USA

- http://www.ibsnewyork.com

Other References:

1. ## Dr. Michael E. Porter (pg 32)

Michael Porter is an economist, researcher, author, advisor, speaker and teacher. Throughout his career at Harvard Business School, he has brought economic theory and strategy concepts to bear on many of the most challenging problems facing corporations, economies and societies, including market competition and company strategy, economic development, the environment, and health care. His extensive research is widely recognized in governments, corporations, NGOs, and academic circles around the globe. His research has received numerous awards, and he is the most cited scholar today in economics and business. While Dr. Porter is, at the core, a scholar, his work has also achieved remarkable acceptance by practitioners across multiple fields

In our business there is not just one "S" word there are many, it's establishing which ones apply and are key to our success.

Remember, we all judge success differently; for me, it is essential to stay creative, be inspired and constantly look for new challenges.

This book has enabled me to do just that.

salon.Shap

Thank you

Mike Vallance

alon.Sur

Success

7.05

CPSIA information can be obtained
at www.ICGtesting.com
Printed in the USA
LVOW05s1813090517

533874LV00004BA/231/P